How We Invented the Airplane

Airplane

An Illustrated History

by ORVILLE WRIGHT

Edited, with an Introduction and Commentary, by
Fred C. Kelly
Additional Text by Alan Weissman

DOVER PUBLICATIONS, INC.
New York

Acknowledgments for the Dover Edition

The publisher gratefully acknowledges the cooperation of Dr. Patrick B. Nolan, Archives and Special Collections, Wright State University, in securing most of the photographs printed in this book. Thanks also to Katherine Bourbeau, photo researcher.

Acknowledgments
[by FRED C. KELLY]

The author of this compilation is much indebted to the aeronautics section of the Library of Congress for help, especially to Marvin W. McFarland, who gave many valuable suggestions. He also received shrewd editorial guidance from Frederick Lewis Allen, editor of *Harper's Magazine*.

Published in Canada by General Publishing Company, Ltd., 30 Lesmill Road, Don Mills, Toronto, Ontario.
Published in the United Kingdom by Constable and Company, Ltd.

This Dover edition, first published in 1988, is an unabridged, greatly enlarged republication of the work first published by the David McKay Company, Inc., New York, 1953 (incorporating a text written in 1920). For further details regarding the contents of the Dover edition, see the Preface.

Drawings by James MacDonald

Manufactured in the United States of America
Dover Publications, Inc.
31 East 2nd Street
Mineola, N.Y. 11501

Library of Congress Cataloging in Publication Data

Wright, Orville, 1871–1948.
    How we invented the airplane : an illustrated history / by Orville Wright ; edited with an introduction and commentary, by Fred C. Kelly ; additional text by Alan Weissman.—Dover ed.
        p.   cm.
    Bibliography: p.
    ISBN 0-486-25662-6
    1. Wright, Wilbur, 1867–1912. 2. Wright, Orville, 1871–1948.
3. Airplanes. I. Kelly, Fred C. (Fred Charters), 1882–1959. II. Title.
TL540.W7A3 1988
629.13′0092′2—dc19
[B]   87-33037
                                                  CIP

Preface to the Dover Edition ——————————

Even from the vantage point of the age of supersonic air travel, the Wright brothers' first flight remains an extraordinary achievement—one without which the development of all practical aircraft would have been very different and probably greatly delayed. Nevertheless, although that crucial moment at 10:35 A.M. on December 17, 1903, near Kitty Hawk, North Carolina, is one of the best-known events of history, very rarely do we get to read in any detail how the Wrights reached that moment or how they perfected their invention in succeeding years. In the Wrights' case, particularly, the details are of supreme importance because, unlike many of their predecessors, they were true scientists and operated not haphazardly but by methodical testing and computation.

Fortunately, the Wrights' invention is one of the best documented of all scientific achievements. On a number of occasions either Orville or Wilbur, or both brothers in collaboration, prepared detailed accounts of their work, in prose that is not only scientifically accurate but clear, lively, and altogether quite readable. In addition,

the brothers were excellent photographers, recording nearly every stage of their experimental and flying activities in hundreds of sharp, well-composed photographs.

The present book is a new compilation of writings about and photographs of the Wrights' invention and their subsequent work in aviation. The central account, to which several other pieces of writing have been attached, is a paper written by Orville in connection with a 1920 legal action. This paper, "How We Invented the Airplane," once thought lost, was discovered after Orville's death by the Wrights' authorized biographer, Fred C. Kelly, and published in a small book in 1953. We have reprinted this book here in its entirety (all omissions, indicated by ellipsis dots, were made for the 1953 book and are given as they appeared there). It includes, besides Orville Wright's paper and another short account by him called "After the First Flights" (presumably also written in or just prior to 1920), three drawings by the distinguished scientific illustrator James MacDonald; an Introduction, a concluding essay "After Kitty Hawk: A Brief Résumé," and liberal commentary, all by Fred Kelly; and several paragraphs written by Wilbur Wright in connection with two earlier legal disputes, one in 1909 and the other in 1912.

In addition, to convey a more complete picture of the Wright brothers' achievements, we have augmented Kelly's book with 76 photographs, most of them taken by Orville or Wilbur Wright. These cover, in greater or lesser detail, almost the whole span of the Wrights' flying experiments from the turn of the century through the time of Wilbur's death in 1912; there are also a few photographs showing their earlier life, as well as a few from Orville's later years. Explanatory captions have been added to the photographs for this edition to supply information not given in the Wrights' accounts or Kelly's commentary. Most of this information has been drawn from standard sources (listed below); in a few cases inferences were made directly from the photographs where information was lacking or the sources seemed mistaken. For example, no one to our knowledge seems to have observed that the Wrights' 1902 glider as rebuilt in 1903 incorporated a new kind of rudder, like that used in the first successful powered airplane.

Finally, we have added as an Appendix an article written by both Wright brothers for the September 1908 issue of *The Century Magazine* (vol. LXXVI, no. 5, pp. 641–50). This piece, probably because it was written closer to the events it describes and because it incorporates Wilbur's as well as Orville's point of view, provides many interesting details about their experiments that Orville fails to mention in his later account. Moreover, it is, in the words of their *Century* editor, "the first popular account of their experiments prepared by the inventors." It also includes a fascinating description of the subjective experience of flying that is almost certainly the first such description ever written by anyone.

The photographs originally "supplied by the authors" for their *Century* article have not been reprinted here. Except for two portraits of the Wrights, they duplicate or are very similar to photographs already included in this compilation. Information given in the *Century* captions has been incorporated into the captions in the present book.

A.W.

Selected Bibliography

Bilstein, Roger E. *Flight in America 1900–1983: From the Wrights to the Astronauts.* Baltimore: The Johns Hopkins University Press, 1984.

Gibbs-Smith, Charles Harvard. *The Wright Brothers: A Brief Account of Their Work, 1899–1911.* London: Her Majesty's Stationery Office, 1963.

Kelly, Fred C. *The Wright Brothers.* New York: Harcourt, Brace and Company, 1943.

Nolan, Patrick B., and Zamonski, John A. *The Wright Brothers Collection: A Guide to the Technical, Business and Legal, Genealogical, Photographic, and Other Archives at Wright State University.* New York: Garland Publishing, 1977.

Renstrom, Arthur G. *Wilbur & Orville Wright Pictorial Materials: A Documentary Guide.* Washington: Library of Congress, 1982.

Villard, Henry Serrano. *Contact! The Story of the Early Birds.* New York: Thomas Y. Crowell Company, 1968.

Contents

Introduction, by FRED C. KELLY   *1*
    Photographs, 1897–ca. 1900   *6*

How We Invented the Airplane, by ORVILLE WRIGHT   *11*
    Photographs, 1900–1903   *22*

After the First Flights, by ORVILLE WRIGHT   *45*
    Photographs, 1904–1905   *47*

After Kitty Hawk: A Brief Résumé, by FRED C. KELLY   *51*
    Photographs, 1908–1940   *56*

Appendix to the Dover Edition:
    The Wright Brothers' Aëroplane,
        by ORVILLE and WILBUR WRIGHT   *81*

Introduction ——————————————————————

by FRED C. KELLY

WHEN WILBUR AND Orville Wright on December 17, 1903, near Kill Devil Hills, North Carolina, made the first flights ever made in a powered, heavier-than-air machine, these brothers dramatized the start of a revolution that has had more effect on the world than anything since the discovery of America. But it did not seem dramatic to them at the time. So great was their faith in their machine that flying it successfully was only what they expected, and they showed no excitement or elation. They knew that the stunt of flying was a minor feat, that their big achievement was *inventing* the machine. They rightly believed that no one but themselves anywhere in the world had the scientific data for building a machine that could fly. By scientific research they had learned the secret.

A mistaken notion is that successful flight had been delayed mainly by lack of efficient light motors. The fact is that the Wrights had solved the greater part of the problem of flight—balance and control, and proper design of wings— in their 1902 glider, with no motor at all. Their first patent is based on that glider. In their gliding in 1902 they could even beat the birds! They measured the angle, with reference to the horizontal, at which the hawks soared, and saw that they themselves could glide at a smaller angle— as small as five and one-third degrees. And yet the equivalent of all the material used in building the 1902 glider had been available to experimenters for hundreds of years. Previous experimenters had lacked only the knowledge of aerodynamic principles that the Wrights had painstakingly gained.

For centuries man had dreamed of flying; but by the time the Wrights became seriously interested in the problem, hope of success was at low ebb. Every attempt to fly had been a failure, and most of the experimenters had quit. As Orville Wright points out farther along in this book, a number of leading scientists had taken the trouble to explain publicly why heavier-than-air flight was impossible. Most experimenters in Europe had accepted that view and turned their attention to steerable balloons. Newspaper readers did not distinguish between a flying-machine

1

and a gas-bag with propellers. Indeed, many editors who had been reading of dirigibles flying over Paris thought the first reports of the Wrights' flights were not worth printing. It was some years before the amazing thing the Wrights had done was taken seriously.

The Wrights not only invented the airplane but had to start the whole process of its proper design almost from scratch. They received surprisingly little help from their predecessors, and what they did receive was more by way of inspiration rather than practical data. Men of high scientific attainments had tackled the flying problem, one of them the great Leonardo da Vinci. A flying-machine built from plans drawn by da Vinci could not possibly have flown. His interest, however, helped to make the study respectable, as did the work, in England, of Sir George Cayley. Early in the 1800's Cayley had published measurements of air pressures for use in building a flying-machine; but they were made on flat planes only, and he considered flat and cambered wings equally good.

It impressed the Wrights that both Clement Ader in France and Dr. Samuel Langley, head of the Smithsonian Institution in Washington, had received large sums from their governments for building flying-machines. Even though the machines were failures, it was evident that trying to fly was not to be thought as crackpot as seeking perpetual motion!

An early experimenter, entitled to greater fame than history gives him, was a Frenchman, Alphonse Pénaud. He was an invalid, who spent much of his life in a wheelchair and died at the age of thirty. But as early as 1871 he had invented various kinds of toy flying machines—both the helicopter type and others that flew horizontally—and he was the originator of the use of twisted rubber bands for motive power in small toys. It was a Pénaud helicopter, given to Wilbur and Orville Wright by their father, when the family was living in Cedar Rapids, Iowa, that first stirred the Wrights' interest in flying machines. Pénaud contrived a system of fore and aft balance for his toys that controlled them in horizontal flight, and the same basic idea is applied in planes today. The Wrights, however, used a method of their own.

Other early experimenters had built small models, but none of them showed enough knowl-

edge of aerodynamic principles to be able to design a successful machine large enough to carry a pilot. A common misconception is that if a man can build a model that flies he should be able to build a larger machine of the same design that would fly equally well. But one difficulty is that when you double the linear measurement of a machine you need about eight times the power to make it fly. Dr. Langley built and flew a model, but his larger machine was a failure. A small boy could build a Pénaud helicopter; but no engineer in the world could build a successful man-carrying machine of the same general design.

The biplane idea had been used long before the Wrights, as far back as early Chinese kites, and a few biplane models even had curved wings; but no one before the Wrights knew what the exact curvature of the wings should be. Nor had any earlier experimenter learned what the aspect ratio (ratio of span to chord) of a wing should be. Moreover, the Wrights were the first to know that there was a loss from having one wing above another, and how much loss.

Greatest of all the forerunners was Otto Lilienthal, a German engineer, father of gliding, who may be called the real inventor of curved surfaces in a flying-machine, since he was the first who could explain in a scientific way why they were superior to flat surfaces. As it turned out, the Lilienthal tables of air pressures on curved surfaces were inaccurate, and the Wrights had to compile tables of their own; but Lilienthal was the Wrights' greatest inspiration. Except for their keen interest in reports of Lilienthal's gliding, it is doubtful if they would ever have started their experiments.

Though the Wrights' first interest in flying-machines came from playing with the Pénaud helicopter, when Wilbur was eleven years old, and Orville seven, and the impression it made on their minds was lasting, it was many years later before they thought of trying to fly. And though they flew kites, as other youngsters did, for the fun of it, it was with no thought of learning how to build a flying-machine.

From early childhood, both Wilbur and Orville Wright were interested in *any* kind of mechanical device. Orville always remembered his fifth birthday, because of a present he received—a gyroscopic top. A little later, after his mother had started him to kindergarten, the family was astonished to learn that, though he left home and returned when he was expected to, he did not go to the kindergarten. Instead, he stopped each morning at the home of a neighbor boy where they could play with an old sewing machine.

Wilbur and Orville may have inherited their pioneering urge and mechanical aptitude. Both traits were in their ancestry. Their mother's father, John G. Koerner, a native of Germany, was so bitterly opposed to German militarism that he migrated to the United States in 1818 and settled near Hillsboro, Virginia, not far from Leesburg. He soon won recognition for the superior quality of the farm wagons and carriages he manufactured. From Virginia he moved to Indiana, at a time when there was still pioneering life in the Hoosier country. Another Wright ancestor, Catharine Van Cleve, was the first white woman to set foot in Dayton, Ohio.

The Wrights' mother, Susan Koerner Wright, had a streak of her father's mechanical ability. She was unusually resourceful in adapting household tools or utensils to unexpected uses and was clever at designing clothes. Her family used to say that "mother could mend anything." She would have been intensely interested in her sons' efforts to design a flying machine, and might even have been helpful, but she died in 1889, a few years before they became seriously interested in the problem.

Their father, Bishop Milton Wright, of the United Brethren Church, whose ancestors were English, was a pioneer in a way. He was born in a log cabin near Rushville, Indiana. After leaving college in Indiana, he spent two years as a teacher at a small college in the Willamette Valley, Oregon, before that region was much settled.

Wilbur Wright was four years older than Orville. They had two older brothers, and a sister, Katharine. She was born exactly three years after Orville. The three older brothers were born in Indiana, Wilbur on a small farm eight miles from New Castle, in April, 1867. Bishop Wright's church duties caused him to be shifted about, and the family moved from Indiana to Dayton, then to Iowa, back to Richmond, Indiana, and finally once more to Dayton. It was during their first stay in Dayton that Orville and Katharine were born. Neither Wilbur nor Orville ever attended college; and, for unusual reasons, neither was

formally graduated from high school, though each attended high school the full time required for a diploma. Wilbur had about finished school in Richmond at the time of the move to Dayton; and to be graduated he would have had to return to Richmond to be present with his class on commencement day. But he did not consider the mere diploma important enough to justify the bother of the trip. He took an extra year in high school at Dayton, studying Greek and trigonometry. When Orville came to his final year in high school, he thought he might wish to go to college and took special studies that included Latin. Though he learned more than if he had followed the prescribed course, he, too, had to do without a diploma.

The Wright household was a harmonious one. Bishop Wright's influence on his sons was great. From their childhood he encouraged them to seek factual information in books, but to do their own thinking. His theological library included books by Robert G. Ingersoll and other agnostics, and he offered no protest when he discovered that Wilbur and Orville were influenced by them. Moreover, he gave his blessing to their spending what money they had on hobbies and experiments. It was all right, he said, to spend money in any way they chose, so long as they earned it. "All the money anyone needs," he said, "is just enough to prevent one from being a burden on others."

Orville once told me that he thought he and Wilbur had enjoyed special advantages. "If my father had not been the kind who encouraged his children to pursue intellectual interests without any thought of profit, our early curiosity about flying would have been nipped too early to bear fruit."

For a time during the brothers' early youth, Wilbur was in poor health, in consequence of being hit in the face with a shinny club while skating; and he seemed reconciled to staying at home, devoting himself to much omnivorous reading. That may explain why Orville seems to have been the one most likely to initiate new lines of activity. They got into the printing business and published fairly profitably the *West Side News.* "I had got interested," Orville told me, "in some woodcuts I saw in the old *Century* magazine, and I tried to make some tools for carving wood blocks. I made my first tool out of the spring of a pocket-knife, and Will fashioned a wooden handle for it. Then we rigged up a crude press, mostly of wood. Finally we got a few fonts of brevier type. It was no fun having a press and type without printing something and finally we began to get out our little neighborhood paper.''

From printing they got into the bicycle business. Their first interest in bicycles was racing; but as their interest grew, they arranged in December, 1892, to start the Wright Cycle Co., to sell, repair, and manufacture bicycles. They opened for business in the spring of 1893.

When they were youngsters, Wilbur naturally treated Orville as a "kid brother," and Orville thought he sometimes did so after they were grown; but there was great devotion and understanding between them. From the time they got into the bicycle business, they always had a joint bank account, and neither paid the slightest attention to what the other drew out for his own use.

In 1895, two years after they started selling bicycles, the Wrights were much interested in an item they chanced to read about the gliding experiments of Lilienthal near Berlin. A year later, when Orville was ill from typhoid fever, Wilbur read that Lilienthal had been killed while gliding. As soon as Orville was well enough for Wilbur to tell him of Lilienthal's death, both became curious to know more of what Lilienthal had done. The idea of gliding through the air appealed to them as sport. Perhaps, they thought, they could begin where Lilienthal left off. They had no notion yet of trying to solve the whole flying problem on their own, least of all with a powered machine. Though they kept thinking of Lilienthal and his work and wondering how much other experimenters had learned, they did not begin serious reading until 1899. Among the books they read was Octave Chanute's *Progress in Flying Machines*. Chanute, a successful engineer, had built the Kansas City bridge and the Chicago stockyards. He was a past president of the American Society of Civil Engineers. As a hobby of his later years he had directed gliding experiments; and his book was the best history of attempts to fly. Wilbur Wright, after reading the book, thought Chanute might be interested in what the Wrights were hoping to do and in May, 1900, wrote to him. That started an exchange of letters which continued for ten years.

Chanute and the Wrights became close friends. From Chanute the Wrights learned more and more of what others had done, and he learned from the Wrights, step by step, how the problem could be solved. He early recognized that the Wrights were far ahead of all others, and once or twice when they thought of dropping their experiments he told them that, in the interest of science, it would be too bad if they quit; that it might be years before anyone else anywhere in the world would know as much about the flying problem as they did, and that he hoped they would go on. He said their work promised "important results." His encouragement to the brothers and his proddings to make them continue were Chanute's great contribution, and it put them deeply in his debt.

When the Wrights were preparing for their second trip to Kitty Hawk, Chanute thought it was highly imprudent for them to make dangerous experiments in so isolated an area, almost hopelessly beyond medical or surgical aid in case of accident. He said he knew a young man named George Spratt of Coatesville, Pennsylvania, an "amateur" in aeronautics, who had had medical training. If the Wrights would board Spratt at their camp, Chanute would pay his railroad fare to the nearest point, and would feel himself compensated by the pleasure given to Spratt. Chanute also asked the Wrights if they would accept as guest, a Tennessean by the name of E. C. Huffaker who had been employed by Chanute in building a glider. The Wrights consented, and so there were four in camp at Kitty Hawk, or rather at Kill Devil Hills, in 1901.

As we approach Orville Wright's own account of how he and his brother invented the airplane, we may wonder just why it was that the Wrights were able to accomplish what for hundreds of years other brilliant men had tried without success. Aside from the fact that each had a superior mind, it may be said that they had the advantage of working together more closely than ordinarily would be possible. Being bachelors, they lived in the same house; and they worked daily in the same shop. They had extraordinary opportunity to discuss the problem and combat each other's ideas until they had agreed upon theories that were sound.

After dinner nearly every night they would sit in the little front parlor at their home on Hawthorne Street in Dayton and argue. Orville was likely to sit erect with arms folded while Wilbur slouched down with his weight mostly on his shoulder blades. Sometimes they would argue so vehemently that Carrie, their housekeeper, would peek in, fearful that they were becoming angry. It was partly in these talks that they invented the airplane.

Though the Wrights often studied the flight of birds in the hope of learning something, they did not at first learn anything of use to them in that way. After they had thought out certain principles, they then watched the birds to see if they used the same principles. As Orville Wright wrote long afterward, "Learning the secret of flight from a bird was a good deal like learning the secret of magic from a magician. After you once know the trick and know what to look for, you see things that you did not notice when you did not know exactly what to look for."

Orville Wright's best account of the process of invention was given in a deposition on January 13, 1920, as witness for the United States Government in a lawsuit. The suit had been brought against the Government by heirs of a man named John Montgomery, to try to show that he had a patent claim that was infringed by airplanes bought by the Government. The Montgomerys lost their case, but the suit served a useful purpose, for it caused Orville Wright to give this best detailed report of how he and his brother succeeded in creating the machine that lifted man into the skies on wings.

For a time, however, it looked as if the almost forgotten deposition might be lost forever. A search of legal records in the Court of Claims in Washington, where the case was tried, proved fruitless. At first it could not be found among the Wright papers deposited in the Library of Congress. Finally a further search there uncovered Orville Wright's typewritten copy.

1. Composite photograph of the Wright family. From left to right: Wilbur, Katharine (sister), Susan Catherine (mother), Lorin (second brother), Milton (father), Reuchlin (eldest brother), Orville.

2. The Wright family occupied this house at 7 Hawthorn Street, Dayton, Ohio, from 1871 to 1878 and then from October 1885 to April 1914, after which they moved to another house in a suburb of Dayton. In 1936 the Hawthorn Street house was moved with Orville's cooperation to the Ford Museum, Greenfield Village, Dearborn, Michigan. (Photograph ca. 1900.)

4

3. The front of the Wright brothers' bicycle shop, 1127 West Third Street, Dayton. They had originally opened their shop at another location nearby in 1892. This was its fourth address and was the site of their important wind-tunnel experiments in 1901. Like the family house, the bicycle shop was moved to Greenfield Village in 1936. (Photograph ca. 1909.)

4. Wilbur at work inside the bicycle shop, 1897. The Wrights manufactured their own bicycles, as well as selling and repairing other models.

How We Invented the Airplane————————

by ORVILLE WRIGHT

OUR FIRST INTEREST [in the problem of flight] began when we were children. Father brought home to us a small toy actuated by a rubber string which would lift itself into the air. We built a number of copies of this toy, which flew successfully. . . . But when we undertook to build a toy on a much larger scale it failed to work so well. The reason for this was not understood by us at the time, so we finally abandoned the experiments. In 1896 we read in the daily papers, or in some of the magazines, of the experiments of Otto Lilienthal, who was making some gliding flights from the top of a small hill in Germany. His death a few months later while making a glide off a hill increased our interest in the subject, and we began looking for books pertaining to flight. We found a work written by Professor Marey on animal mechanism which treated of the bird mechanism as applied to flight, but other than this, so far as I can remember, we found little.

In the spring of 1899 our interest in the subject was again aroused through the reading of a book on ornithology. We could not understand that there was anything about a bird that would enable it to fly that could not be built on a larger scale and used by man. At this time our thought pertained more particularly to gliding flight and soaring. If the bird's wings would sustain it in the air without the use of any muscular effort, we did not see why man could not be sustained by the same means. We knew that the Smithsonian Institution had been interested in some work on the problem of flight, and, accordingly, on the 30th of May 1899, my brother Wilbur wrote a letter to the Smithsonian inquiring about publications on the subject. Several days later we received a letter signed by R. Rathbun, assistant secretary.

Among the reprints of the Smithsonian sent to us and mentioned in the letter was the *Problem of Flying and Practical Experiments in Soaring*, by Otto Lilienthal; *Story of Experiments in Mechanical Flight*, by S. P. Langley; and, I think, a paper by Pettigrew, as well as a copy of Mouillard's *Empire of the Air*. We sent for copies of Chanute's *Progress in Flying Machines*, Langley's *Experiments in Aerodynamics*, and the Aeronautical

Annuals of 1895, 1896, and 1897. On reading the different works on the subject we were much impressed with the great number of people who had given thought to it—among these some of the greatest minds the world has produced. But we found that the experiments of one after another had failed. Among these who had worked on the problem I may mention Leonardo da Vinci, one of the greatest artists and engineers of all time; Sir George Cayley, who was among the first of the inventors of the internal-combustion engine; Sir Hiram Maxim, inventor of the Maxim rapid-fire gun; Parsons, the inventor of the turbine steam engine; Alexander Graham Bell, inventor of the telephone; Horatio Phillips, a well-known English engineer; Otto Lilienthal, the inventor of instruments used in navigation and a well-known engineer; Thomas A. Edison; and Dr. S. P. Langley, secretary and head of the Smithsonian Institution. Besides these there were a great number of other men of ability who had worked on the problem. But the subject had been brought into disrepute by a number of men of lesser ability who had hoped to solve the problem through devices of their own invention which had all of them failed, until finally the public was led to believe that flying was as impossible as perpetual motion. In fact scientists of the standing of Guy-Lussac, the great French scientist and engineer, and Professor Simon Newcomb, one of the greatest of the American scientists and mathematicians, had attempted to prove that it would be impossible to build a flying machine that would carry a man. Admiral Melville, chief engineer in the United States Navy, a little later, in 1901, or 1902, published an article in which he pointed out the difficulties of building a flying machine to carry a man, and stated that the first flying machine would be more expensive than the most costly battleship.

After reading the pamphlets sent to us by the Smithsonian we became highly enthusiastic with the idea of gliding as a sport. We found that Lilienthal had been killed through his inability to properly balance his machine in the air. Pilcher, an English experimenter, had met with a like fate.

We found that both of these experimenters had attempted to maintain balance merely by the shifting of the weight of their bodies. Chanute, and I believe all the other experimenters before 1900, used this same method of maintaining the equilibrium in gliding flight. We at once set to work to devise a more efficient means of maintaining the equilibrium. . . .

The first method that occurred to us for maintaining the lateral equilibrium was that of pivoting the wings on the right and left sides on shafts carrying gears at the center of the machine, which, being in mesh, would cause one wing to turn upward in front when the other wing was turned downward. By this method we thought it would be possible to get a greater lift on one side than on the other, so that the shifting of weight would not be necessary for the maintenance of balance. However, we did not see any method of building this device sufficiently strong and at the same time light enough to enable us to use it.

A short time afterward, one evening when I returned home with my sister and Miss Harriet Silliman, who was at that time a guest of my sister's in our home, Wilbur showed me a method of getting the same results as we had contemplated in our first idea without the structural defects of the original. He demonstrated the method by means of a small pasteboard box, which had . . . the opposite ends removed. By holding the top forward corner and the rear lower corner of one end of the box between his thumb and forefinger and the rear upper corner and the lower forward corner of the other end of the box in the like manner, and by pressing the corners together, the upper and lower surface of the box were given a helicoidal [*spiral*] twist, presenting the top and bottom surfaces of the box at different angles on the right and left sides.

From this it was apparent that the wings of a machine of the Chanute double-deck type, with the fore-and-aft trussing removed, could be warped in like manner, so that, in flying, the wings on the right and left sides could be warped so as to present their surfaces to the air at different angles of incidence and thus secure unequal lifts on the two sides. . . .[1]

We began the construction of a model embodying the principle demonstrated with the paper box within a day or two. This model consisted of

---

[1]Courts have held that the Wrights, as pioneers, had priority on *any* method for presenting the right and left wings at different angles. They had discovered the aileron principle.

superposed planes each measuring five feet from tip to tip and about thirteen inches from front to rear. The model was built and, as I remember it, was tested in the latter part of July 1899. . . . I was not myself present. . . .

[*Experiments with this five-foot apparatus, more a model glider than a kite, were confined to one day.*]

According to Wilbur's account of the tests, the model worked very successfully. It responded promptly to the warping of the surfaces, always lifting the wing that had the larger angle. Several times . . . when he shifted the upper surface backward by the manipulation of the sticks attached to flying cords, the nose of the machine turned downward as was intended, but in diving downward it created a slack in the flying cords, so that he was not able to control it further. The model made such a rapid dive to the ground that the small boys present fell on their faces to avoid being hit, not having time to run. . . .

We felt that the model had demonstrated the efficiency of our system of control. After a little time we decided to experiment with a man-carrying machine embodying the principle of lateral control used in the kite model already flown. From the tables of Lilienthal we calculated that a machine having an area of a little over 150 square feet would support a man when flown in a wind of sixteen miles an hour. We expected to fly the machine as a kite and in this way we thought we would be able to stay in the air for hours at a time, getting in this way a maximum of practice with a minimum of effort. In September of 1900 we went to Kitty Hawk,[2] North Carolina, and there assembled the machine, most of the parts of which we had made at Dayton.

From the United States Weather Bureau reports we had found that Kitty Hawk was one of the windiest places in the country, and that during the month of September it had an average wind in the neighborhood of 16 miles an hour. We wrote to the Weather Bureau man at the Kitty Hawk station, telling him of the nature of

the experiments we wished to conduct and asking him in regard to the suitability of the ground in that neighborhood. We received a very favorable report from him, and also from the postmaster at Kitty Hawk, to whom he had shown our letter.

[The machine] had two superposed surfaces measuring eighteen feet from tip to tip and about five feet from front to rear. The surfaces were spaced five feet apart and were connected at the extreme forward edge by six upright posts, and at about one foot from the rear edge by another row of uprights or struts. The struts were connected to the surfaces by means of flexible joints. The ribs were made of thin strips of ash, slightly bent near their forward extremities. These ribs were bound to the forward spar on the spar's upper side, so that the spar and curvature given to the ribs produced a [wing] curvature of about one-eighteenth to one-twentieth of the chord [the straight-line distance from front to rear edge of wing]. The spars were enclosed in a sheath formed by sewing a strip of cloth over them, resulting in the elimination of all sharp angles or corners. The ribs were enclosed likewise.

Both the forward and the rear rows of uprights were trussed by wires much like the Chanute glider. The machine thus had two systems of rigid trusses laterally; but, unlike the Chanute machine, it was not rigidly trussed from front to rear. On the contrary, a flexible cable was connected to the upper surface at the extreme outer upright in the rear, passed diagonally downward through a pulley on the lower surface at the outermost forward upright, thence across to a pulley in a corresponding position on the lower plane on the opposite side of the machine, and then diagonally upward to a connection to the upper surface at the outermost rear upright. Another flexible cable was attached to the upper surface at its forward edge at the outermost upright on the one side, passed diagonally downward and backward and crossing the first-mentioned flexible cable to a pulley at the rear of the lower surface, then across to a pulley at the rear of the lower surface at the opposite side, and then up to the connection of the forward upright to the upper surface. A cradle in which the operator lay was connected to the cable running along the forward edge of the lower surface, so that when the

---

[2]Natives around Kitty Hawk showed only mild interest in the Wrights' hopes of flying, but they became much excited when they learned that the brothers had sent to Elizabeth City, fifty miles away, for a barrel of gasoline and intended to keep the highly explosive stuff right in their tent. Didn't these men know how dangerous it was? Mothers cautioned their children not to go near the tent. The Wrights wanted the gasoline not for a motor but for their cookstove. It was the first gasoline ever taken to the Kitty Hawk area.

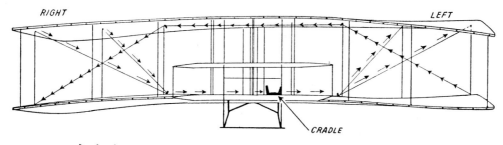

RIGHT LEFT

CRADLE

→ → → CABLES ATTACHED TO CRADLE — SLIDING CRADLE TO LEFT
OF MACHINE PULLS TRAILING EDGE OF RIGHT WING DOWNWARD

⟶ ⟶ CABLE (NOT ATTACHED TO CRADLE) IS MOVED
AUTOMATICALLY BY DOWNWARD MOVEMENT OF RIGHT WING

[*The accompanying picture of the Wrights' first powered machine (with motor and propellers removed) shows the method of twisting the rear of the wings. A movement of only an inch or two, to right or left, of the operator's hips resting on the little cradle was enough to give greater lift to whichever wing needed it, and to restore sidewise balance.*

And here is Wilbur Wright's own explanation, given as witness in the suit of The Wright Company against Glenn H. Curtiss and the Herring-Curtiss Company, of how the Wright system of control was used in making circular turns.]

In order to circle to the left, we moved the cradle slightly to the left, thus turning the tail slightly to the left and imparting an increased angle to the right wing and a smaller angle to the left wing. This caused the machine to tilt so that the left wing was lower than the right wing, which, of course, in turn, caused the machine to slide somewhat to the left. This side movement of the machine tended to cause the vertical rudder to strike the air at a greater angle than was necessary to compensate for the difference in resistance of the right and left wings.

This tendency caused the tail to lag behind in this lateral movement just as the feather of an arrow causes the feathered end to lag behind when the arrow is dropped sidewise. Thus the lateral movement of the main aeroplane

sidewise, as the result of tipping, became combined with the rotary movement about its vertical axis, due to the vane-like action of the tail, and the machine proceeded on a circular course. But as the speed of the outside wing increased, and that of the inside wing decreased, by reason of the fact that the inner wing was traveling in a smaller circle than the outside wing, there was a tendency to tilt too much and this was corrected by gradually moving the cradle toward the high wing, thus increasing the angle on the low wing and decreasing the angle of the high wing and also setting the rudder over toward the high wing. This was done gradually, but only sufficiently to prevent the low wing from sinking lower and not enough to bring it back to the level. The machine then continued to circle to the left, with the vertical tail set over somewhat to the right, so that the machine turned in the opposite direction to that in which a ship would have turned with the ship's rudder set over to the right.

When it was desired to stop circling, a sudden movement of the cradle toward the high side gave the wings an increased warp and brought the machine up to the level. Then on setting the cradle back to its central position, thus restoring the wings and tail to their central positions, the machine proceeded in a straight line, with the wings level.

cable was pushed to the right the upper rear corner of the machine was pulled downward and forward and the corresponding part on the opposite side of the machine was allowed to move upward and rearward. In this manner a helicoidal warp was imparted to the surfaces.

The horizontal rudder, or elevator, was attached to a framework about four feet forward of the lower main plane. This elevator was pivoted about one-third back from its front edge. To the forward edge of the elevator were attached two springs which extended horizontally forward to the framework which supported the elevator. The rear edge of the elevator could be raised or lowered by means of two arms extending from the operator and connecting to the rear edge of the elevator through links. Thus when the rear edge of the elevator was raised, the springs referred to

prevented the front edge from moving downward to a like angle, and as a result a curvature was given to the elevator on its upper side. When the rear edge of the elevator was moved downward a curvature on the under side was produced. . . .[3]

We attempted to fly the machine as a kite with a man on board a number of times, but were successful in keeping it up only when the wind was about twenty-five miles or more an hour. It failed to perform in lifting as had been calculated from the Lilienthal tables of air pressure. However, when flown in the strong winds, it responded promptly to the warping of the wings, so that the side with the greater angle would rise above the side with the lower angle and the machine

[3]The front elevator in the first power plane was operated differently.

would go sidling off toward the lower side, but the low side was brought up again by reversing the angles of the wing tips.

We also made a number of tests of it flown without an operator in which we attempted to measure the lift, the drift, and the center of pressure.

Before leaving camp for the year we carried it to the Kill Devil Hill, four miles from Kitty Hawk, and made about a dozen free flights, gliding down the side of the hill on the air. . . . The experiments were concluded near the end of October. . . .

Although we were highly pleased with the performance of the machine, in so far as lateral control was concerned, we were disappointed with its lifting ability. We did not know whether its failure to lift according to the calculations made previous to our going to Kitty Hawk was due to the construction of our machine, or whether the tables of air pressure, at that time generally accepted, were incorrect. As a result we wrote to Mr. Chanute soon after our return from Kitty Hawk, giving him an account of the experiments just made, and asking his opinion as to the cause of the failure of the machine to lift, according to calculations. He suggested that it might have been due to the peculiar shape of wing curvature which we had used, and recommended that if we took up experiments again we use ribs having curvature used by Lilienthal. . . .

In order to try to satisfy our own minds as to whether the failure of the 1900 machine to lift according to our calculations was due to the shape of the wings or to an error in the Lilienthal tables,

we undertook a number of experiments to determine the comparative lifting qualities of planes as compared with curved surfaces and the relative value of curved surfaces having different depths of curvature. This was done by mounting the two surfaces to be compared at the extremities of the arms of an acute V-shaped structure made of wood. The V was pivoted on a vertical bearing at its point, the V lying in a horizontal plane. The surfaces were mounted vertically on the V, with their lifts opposed to each other. In this way we attempted to determine which had the greater lift by the amount one surface could push the other from the normal position. The surfaces while so mounted were exposed to the wind. The experiments were so crudely carried out that close measurements were not possible. But the results of these experiments confirmed us in the belief already formed that the accepted tables of air pressure were not to be altogether relied upon.

It was for this reason that we decided to increase the size of the machine of 1901, as well as to make the ribs and wings of a deeper curvature fore and aft. The 1901 machine was assembled at Kitty Hawk or, rather, near the Kill Devil Hill, in July 1901. The structure was very similar to that of the previous year. The method of imparting a helicoidal warp to the wings used in 1900 was used again in 1901. The area of the wings was increased from 165 square feet of the 1900 machine to 290 square feet, the wings having a spread of twenty-two feet, and a chord of seven feet. The depth of curvature of the wings was increased to one-twelfth of the chord, the deepest point being about 33 per cent back. . . .

This machine was tested a number of times in free gliding flight and also as a kite. In the gliding flights the fore-and-aft stability or control of the machine did not seem to be as good as that of the previous year. This we finally suspected was due to the difference in the curvature of the wings of the two machines. We also found that where the machine of 1900 continued to increase in speed as we glided down certain slopes of the hill, the 1901 machine did not do so. This seemed to indicate that the machine of 1900 was able to glide on slopes of less angle than the machine of 1901, and was therefore dynamically more efficient. The lateral control of the new machine appeared very effective. As a result of these experiments we soon decided to reduce the curvature of the wings, which we did by a system of

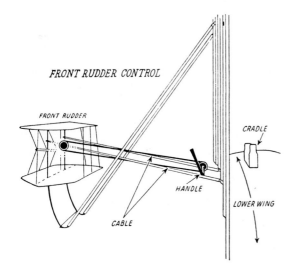

FRONT RUDDER CONTROL

FRONT RUDDER

CRADLE

HANDLE

LOWER WING

CABLE

posts and wires about midway between the front and rear spars.

These intermediate posts also served to prevent the ribs and wings from taking a deeper curvature due to the air pressure upon them. It had been found that the curvature of the wings was constantly changing during flight. The machine as thus modified was flown a number of times in gliding flights and as a kite with and without an operator on board. A number of measurements were made of the machine flown as a kite to determine the lift and the drift at various angles of incidence. The results obtained did not agree at all with the estimated values computed from Lilienthal and other accepted tables of air pressure. . . .

As we gained in proficiency in handling the machine in gliding flight, we began to encounter occasionally a phenomenon which we had not foreseen. Sometimes in warping the wings to recover lateral balance, it was found that the wing having the greater angle would at first tend to lift, but at the same time it would lose speed as compared with the opposite wing having a smaller angle of incidence.[4] As a result the machine would begin turning a sharp circle, which generally resulted in a forced landing with the machine skidding outward on the ground. From this phenomenon we were led to the discovery that the relative velocities of the right and left wings of the machine bore a very important part in lateral equilibrium, a fact apparently never before considered by any investigators. I may state that in some of the flights just related, the wing having

the larger angle and the lesser speed had a less lift than the other wing with the small angle and the greater speed.

The measurements of lift and drift, which were made in this year and the year before, I believe, were the first that were ever made upon a full-sized model; and I believe these were the first adequate tests that had ever been made, as to the accuracy of the accepted tables of air pressures.

We made a great number of measurements of the machine used as a glider. We accurately measured with a clinometer the angle of the machine's descent. With a Richard hand anemometer we measured the velocity of the wing at the height from the ground, when possible, at which the flight was made. The time during which the machine was in free flight was measured with a stop watch. The distance of the free flight over the ground was also measured. In many flights the speed of the machine relative to the air was measured by a man running beside the machine holding an anemometer in his hand. From the angle of descent as measured with the clinometer the ratio of the total lift of the machine to its total resistance can be easily and accurately computed.

We also made a number of measurements with the machine flying as a kite, sometimes empty and sometimes loaded with a bag of sand. These measurements were taken by measuring the pull on the flying cables at the two ends of the machine, when these cables were in a horizontal position so that the pull of the cables would neither add to nor detract from the load carried by the machine. As an example I will give a few

---

[4]In another lawsuit Wilbur Wright, in February, 1912, a little more than three months before his death, explained the angle of incidence as follows:

The angle of incidence of an aeroplane is the angle at which the aeroplane surfaces and the air stream meet. It may or may not correspond with the angle of the aeroplane with the horizon. This angle, that is, the angle of incidence, is continually varying in flight in accordance with the speed of the machine. If the speed is low, a large angle of incidence is required to sustain the machine. If the speed is high, a small angle of incidence suffices to sustain the machine. When the machine is climbing to a greater height, the power of the motor is expended in lifting the weight. Consequently there is less power to drive the machine forward and the speed is less in this case, but the angle of incidence greater. Similar variations in the angle of incidence occur whenever the machine meets an air current of greater velocity or less velocity, or if the current has an upward or downward trend. If the load carried by the aeroplane is decreased, which normally happens by the consumption of oil and fuel, the angle of incidence decreases. If from any cause the power of the motor decreases, the angle of incidence increases. If an extra passenger is carried, the angle of incidence is greater than usual through-

out the flight. If the air, from some cause, has a greater upward trend in one place than in another, the angle of incidence on one wing will be greater than the angle of incidence on the other wing. From these various causes the actual angle of incidence is, under normal conditions, an angle sometimes above and sometimes below the average angle which defendants refer to as the normal angle of incidence. It is very rarely that the machine flies, even for a short time, at the exact angle which they call the normal angle of incidence. More than 90 per cent of the time the machine is flying at some other angle. When the variations in the angle of incidence are produced by variations in load, variations in regard to ascent or descent, or by variations in the power of the motor, the variations in the angle of incidence continue for many minutes or even hours. In rapid climbing the angle of incidence of aeroplanes is usually ten degrees or more, that is, machines usually climb fastest when the forward speed is rather slow and the angle of incidence great, because then less power is expended in driving the machine forward and more is available for climbing. The angle of incidence which any particular machine normally utilizes in its work varies all the way from about 2½ degrees up to nearly 15 degrees.

measurements made on July 30, 1901. Wind velocity, 18 miles per hour; angle of incidence, 10°; lift, 100 pounds; drift, 18 pounds. Another set of measurements made on August 1, 1901, after the machine had been slightly modified, were as follows: Velocity, 17 miles per hour; angle of incidence, 6°; weight, 100 pounds; drift, 15 pounds. These measurements show a lift of about one-third of the estimates that had been made using the Lilienthal tables of air pressure.

Several hundred fights were made [in 1901]. I do not know the exact number. The flights ranged all the way from fifty feet to nearly four hundred feet in length. Quite a number were made of a distance of three hundred feet or more.

Changes in the arrangement of the spars were made several times during the series of experiments, the most important of which was produced by changing the length of the brace wires, so as to produce a curvature in the spars from wing to wing. The spars at the center of the machine were raised three or four inches above their extremities at the wing tips. The spars when the machine was first assembled were straight, the diagonal brace wires in each section being of equal lengths.

We had found in the free flights that when the wind entered the machine from one side or the other at an angle to the longitudinal axis of the machine, the wing on that side from which the wind was blowing received a greater lift, thus causing a disturbance in the lateral equilibrium of the machine. By giving the wings a curvature from side to side this disturbance was avoided, because the air entering from the side met the surface of the wing on that side at a smaller angle of incidence than it met the surface on the opposite wing. This, however, tends to produce a machine with unstable equilibrium laterally. While the equilibrium is disturbed less from side gusts, the machine tends to lose its own equilibrium when it slips sidewise on the air, but under the peculiar conditions existing on the Kill Devil Hill [partly the hill's convex surface] we found the advantages of the drooped wings more than overcame the disadvantages.

All the books and papers which my brother and I had read in which there was any reference to the travel of the center of pressure had taught that the center of pressure was approximately at the center of the surface when it was exposed at right angles to the wind; and that this center of pressure moved forward as the angle of incidence was decreased. We had built both the 1900 and the 1901 machines assuming this to be well verified. Our elevator was placed in front of the surfaces with the idea of producing inherent stability fore and aft, which it should have done had the travel of the center of pressure been forward as we had been led to believe. We found, however, that these machines were anything but inherently stable fore and aft. In our 1900 experiments we had even found the inherent stability much improved when we tested the machine by gliding it down a hill loaded with a small sack of sand with the trailing edge of the main plane forward and the elevator trailing behind [*in short, when flying it backward*].

Doctor Spratt and Mr. Huffaker [then staying at the Wright camp] both suggested that there might be a rearward travel of the center of pressure on the curved surfaces at the small angles of incidence. We later demonstrated this fact by flying one of the surfaces alone as a kite. When the surface was exposed to the wind at large angles of incidence the pull on the flying cords was upward and when exposed at small angles of incidence the pull was downward. In the first case it was apparent that the center of pressure was in front of the center of gravity, and in the latter case behind the center of gravity. This clearly demonstrated that the center of pressure moved backward at small angles of incidence. . . .

Our experiments of 1901 were rather discouraging to us because we felt that they had demonstrated that some of the most firmly established laws, those regarding the travel of the center of pressure and pressures on airplane surfaces, were mostly, if not entirely, incorrect. At first we had taken up the problem merely as a matter of sport, but now it was apparent that if we were to make much progress it would be necessary to get better tables from which to make our calculations. In September we set up a small wind tunnel in which we made a number of measurements similar to those which we had attempted to make earlier in the year. The earlier measurements had been made in the open air, where it was difficult to determine the exact direction of the wind. The new measurements were made inside of the tunnel, through which a blast of air was forced. The new experiments were conducted with much more care than had been the first, but still they were not entirely satisfactory. We immediately set about designing and constructing another apparatus from which we hoped to secure much more accurate measurements. In this instrument the lift of the surface to be measured was balanced against a pressure created on a screen by the flow of the air through the tunnel. This enabled us to make very accurate comparative measurements of the lift.

We also designed and constructed another instrument for measuring the ratio of the lift to the drift. This utilized an idea which had been suggested by Dr. Spratt. During the following three or four months after October 1901 we made thousands of measurements of the lift, and the ratio of the lift to the drift with these two instruments. We measured the lift of square planes and rectangular planes of different aspect ratios, in order to determine the effect of the aspect ratio on the lifting qualities of the plane. We also made measurements of a number of similarly curved surfaces having different cambers to determine the effect of camber on the lift and also on the drift.

We also measured these curved surfaces to determine the effect of aspect ratio on their lifts and drifts. We measured a number of surfaces superposed with gaps ranging from one-fourth of the chord to one and one-eighth times the chord. We measured a series of surfaces having a regular camber like that of a sector of cylinder, [and] having different depths of curvature, as well as a great number of other surfaces having the greatest depth of curvature forward of the center, and some with the greatest depth back of the center. . . .

We decided to build another machine basing it upon calculations to be made from our own tables. We decided to attach a fixed vertical vane in the rear of the main plane, which we thought would maintain an equal velocity of the right and left wings when the wings were warped to different angles. Our tables made it apparent that we would secure a higher dynamic efficiency in the machine by using surfaces of smaller camber and of greater aspect ratio.

We went to Kitty Hawk in the last week of August 1902, and began the assembling of a machine embodying the changes which I have just mentioned. The wings of this machine measured 32 feet from tip to tip, and 5 feet from front to rear. The curvature of the wings measured from one twenty-fourth to one twenty-sixth of the chord of the surfaces. The front rudder, or elevator, contained 15 square feet of surface, and the rear vertical vanes had a total surface of 11⅔ square feet. The area of the main planes totaled 305 square feet. These planes were spaced one 5 feet above the other. The wiring or trussing of the wings and uprights, as well as the arrangement of the cables for imparting the warp to the surfaces, was like that of the 1901 machine. The arrangement of the trussing and the method of producing the warp in the surfaces is clearly shown in Figure 1 of the Wright patent of May 22, 1906.

While this machine was being assembled, we made measurements of one of the surfaces flown as a kite, and found that the pull on the kite strings, in proportion to the load carried, was less than that of the surfaces of the 1901 machine. This was in accordance with the estimates which we had made from calculations based on our own tables. These measurements were taken when the kite strings stood in a horizontal position, so that only the drift of the surface was measured.

The assembling of the machine was completed about the 19th of September, when we began making glides with it. . . . In the first flight we found that the machine was able to glide with a much smaller angle of descent than either of our former machines. The first glides made with it, but which were not entirely free, led us to think that the lateral control had been improved by the addition of the fixed vertical vanes in the rear. In these first tests the wing with the larger angle would rise, while the opposite wing was depressed.

This machine was assembled with the spars straight from tip to tip, but as these first tests showed the same trouble that we had had with the 1901 machine when the wings were straight, on the 22nd of September we altered the truss wire so as to arch the surfaces from tip to tip, making the tips at least four inches lower than the center. We also made the angle of the surfaces at the tips greater than the angle at the center of the machine. We found that the trouble experienced before with a cross wind turning up the wing it first struck had been overcome, and the trials seemed to indicate that with an arch to the surfaces laterally the opposite effect was obtained.

Later, when we began to make free flights with the machine, we found that when the wings were warped, first with the larger angle on one side and then on the other, the machine descended the hill rolling from side to side. But later in some of the flights, when the machine was allowed to slide a little to one side or the other as the result of one wing being at an almost imperceptibly lower height than the other, we found that the fixed vertical vane, instead of maintaining an equal speed at the two opposite wing tips, as we had expected, as a matter of fact did just the reverse, and caused one wing to be checked and the other one to be speeded up. This was due to the fact that when the machine began sliding laterally a pressure was created on the fixed vanes on that side which was toward the lower side of the machine and the side toward which the machine was sliding. The increased speed of the high wing gave it a still greater lift, and the decreased speed of the lower wing produced a lesser lift upon it, with the result that the lower wing dropped and the higher wing went still higher. When the wings were warped in an attempt to recover balance, with the low wing having a greater angle of incidence than the upper wing, a still greater drag was produced upon the low wing, with a result that its speed was further decreased and the speed of the higher wing was increased. These flights ended usually with disaster to the machine in what is called today a "tail spin." . . .

Our first change in the machine, as the result of our experiences in these flights just mentioned, was to remove one of the vertical vanes in the rear of the machine. By doing this we hoped to remove at least a part of the disturbing effect of the vanes when the machine was sliding slightly sidewise. We found that this only slightly mitigated the evil influence of vanes. After a good deal of thought the idea occurred to us that by making the vane in the rear adjustable, so that it could be turned, . . . to entirely relieve the pressure on that side toward the low side of the machine, and to create a pressure on the side toward the high wing equal to or greater than the differences in the resistances of the high and low wings, due to their different angles of incidence, all of the good properties of a vane in the rear would be secured without any of its bad properties. But this was going to add one more burden to the operator. He would now not only have to think, and think quickly, in operating the front elevator for maintaining the longitudinal equilibrium, but

REAR RUDDER CONTROL

—·—·— REAR RUDDER CABLES
THESE CABLES ARE ATTACHED TO THE
WING-WARPING CABLES AND LEAD TO REAR RUDDER

he would also have to think so as to operate this rudder . . . to present its surface to the wind on that side which is toward the high wing, or the wing having the smaller angle of incidence.

While this change to make the vane adjustable was being made, the idea came to us of connecting the wires which operated the rudder to the cables which operated the wing warping, so that whenever the wings were warped the rudder was simultaneously adjusted, . . . to produce a pressure on that side of the rudder which was toward the wing having the smaller angle of incidence. [*Later the Wrights found it desirable, through the experimental stage, to operate the wings and rudder separately.*]

With the machine as now constituted we began a long series of gliding flights. The disastrous experiences which we had when the fixed vanes were used now seemed to be entirely avoidable. In fact, in the seven or eight hundred gliding flights that were made after the adjustable rudder was installed, not once did we encounter the difficulty we had experienced with the fixed vane. . . .

The fore-and-aft control of the 1902 machine had proved very effective, so that when at last we felt that the problem of lateral equilibrium had been entirely solved, we began to turn our thoughts to the construction of a machine to be driven with a motor. . . . To provide for the installation of motor, propellers, etc., we thought a more rigid structure at the center of the machine would be useful. As a result we decided to rigidly truss the upper and lower planes of this 1902 machine in all excepting the outermost panel at each end. This was accomplished by putting in fore-and-aft stay wires, running diagonally from the upper end of the forward upright posts to the lower end of the corresponding rear posts, and from the upper end of the rear posts to the lower end of the corresponding front upright posts. In this manner we provided a rigid structure in the three center panels. Before this modification was made, in warping the wings, the upper and lower surfaces were drawn into diagonal positions with reference to each other. With the new form of trussing, the front edges of the upper and lower planes were maintained parallel to each other, so that only the rear edges of the outer panels at either end of the machine could be adjusted up and down for the purpose of securing different angles of incidence at the two opposite tips.

All of the later flights made with this machine in 1902, as well as the early flights made with it in 1903, were made with the wings trussed in the manner just described.

The flights of 1902 demonstrated the efficiency of our system of control for both longitudinal and lateral stability. They also demonstrated that our tables of air pressure which we made in our wind tunnel would enable us to calculate in advance the performance of a machine. Before leaving our camp at Kitty Hawk we began the designing of a new and larger machine to be driven by motor. The wings of the new machine had a spread of 40 feet 6 inches and a chord of 6 feet 6 inches, having a total area of a little over 500 square feet.

Immediately after our return from Kitty Hawk in 1902 we wrote to a number of the best-known automobile manufacturers in an endeavor to secure a motor for the new machine. Not receiving favorable answers from any of these, we proceeded to design a motor of our own, from which we hoped to secure about 8 horsepower. When the motor was tested it gave more power than we had anticipated. It developed a little over 12 horsepower and weighed about 160 pounds, without magneto, water, or oil.

We next proceeded with the construction of the parts to be used in this first power machine, and while we were doing this we began an investigation of screw propellers. At first we hoped to be able to procure a theory of the reactions on a screw propeller from works on marine engineering, but we soon found, after examining the few books we were able to secure in the Dayton Public Library pertaining to marine engineering, that water screw propellers at that time were not based upon theory but almost entirely upon empirical data. We had thought that we could adopt the theory from the marine engineers, and then by using our tables of air pressures, instead of the tables of water pressures used in their calculations, that we could estimate in advance the performance of the propellers we would use. When we found we could not do this, we began the study of the screw propeller from an entirely theoretical standpoint, since we saw that with the small capital we possessed we would not be able to develop an efficient air propeller on the "cut and try" plan. As a result of this study we developed a theory from which we designed the propellers which we used in this 1903 power machine.

These propellers had an efficiency of over 66 per cent, an efficiency, I believe, rarely exceeded by the marine engineers, and never approached by any of the aeronautical investigators up to that time. . . .

We went to Kitty Hawk the latter part of September 1903, and after a few days spent in establishing camp and in erecting a building in which to assemble and house our new machine, we began the work of assembling. . . . While in general the structure of these wings was similar to that of the previous gliding machines which we had built, yet a number of changes in design were made, among which I may mention that of the ribs and the covering of the surface with cloth. Instead of using thin strips of ash, bent to the desired curvature, as had been used in the earlier machines, for the new machine the ribs were made by [sawing] a piece of ash, with a cross section of about three-eighths by one-half inch, . . . from one end to within a few inches of the other, inserting blocks of wood between the two halves of the strip and gluing and nailing them in position. . . . Through this structure we secured at the same time great strength and lightness. Ribs of this type are used in practically all flying machines today. The cloth was stretched over both the top and bottom sides of the spars and ribs.

These, I believe, were the first double-surfaced planes ever designed or built. . . . The control of this machine was the same as that of the 1902 machine. Like the 1902 machine in the later part of the season, the central portions remained fixed, while the outer portions of the wings were adjusted to different angles of incidence. . . .

The first attempt to fly this machine was made on the 14th of December, but through a mistake in handling it at the start the machine was broken slightly, so that repairs had to be made before another attempt could be undertaken. Five men from the Kill Devil Life Saving Station were present when this test was made. . . . The next trial was made on the 17th of December, in a wind blowing 20 miles, and four more flights were made. The first of these covered a distance of about 100 feet, measured from the end of the track, and had a duration of about 12 seconds. The second and third flights covered about 175 feet, and the fourth flight 852 feet. This last flight had a duration of 59 seconds.

These flights started from a point about 100 feet to the west of our camp. The ground was perfectly level for a mile or two in every direction excepting those toward the big and the smaller Kill Devil Hills. The ground was level in the directions toward these hills for a distance of a quarter of a mile.

The machine was launched from a monorail track. . . . This track was laid in a slight depression, which a few days before had been covered by water. We chose this spot because the action of the water had leveled it so nearly flat that little preparation of the ground was necessary in order to lay the track. The starting end of the track lay a few inches below the end from which the machine lifted into the air.

A small two-wheeled truck ran on the track. Across the truck extended a beam, upon the two opposite ends of which the skids of the machine rested. A bicycle hub was attached at the forward end of the skids, beneath the elevator. This supported the forward end of the machine and guided the machine on a rail.

The machine was launched entirely through the power of the motor and the thrust of the propellers.

In the last flight the rate of travel over the ground was approximately 10 miles per hour against a wind of approximately 20 miles per hour, making the real speed of the machine through the air about 30 miles an hour.

The first of these flights . . . was the first time in the history of the world that a machine carrying a man and driven by a motor had lifted itself from the ground in free flight.

Witnesses of this flight, besides my brother and myself, were John T. Daniels, W. S. Dough, A. D. Etheridge, from the Kill Devil Life Saving Station; W. C. Brinkley, of Manteo; and Johnny Moore, a boy from Nags Head, North Carolina.

[*Devices for obtaining records of the time, the distance through the air, and the engine speed, were arranged almost as ingeniously as the machine itself. An anemometer, a revolution counter, and a stop watch, all of which started and stopped simultaneously, were installed on the machine.*

One little disappointment was that the jar of rough landings set the stop watch back to zero. That happened in all four flights on December 17. However, the time in the air of each flight was independently timed by another stop watch held by the brother who stayed at the starting point.

It may be added that the obtaining of a good picture of the first flight was not accidental. The single-rail starting track was 60 feet long, but the brothers knew that with a wind of more than 20 miles an hour they would not need to run to the end of the rail before taking off. For each flight the plane left the rail at the moment the pilot turned the wings to a flying angle, and on the first trial that moment came after the plane had gone only two-thirds the length of the rail. Orville Wright estimated accurately what he was going to do, and had set his camera, for another man to operate, aimed at just the right place to catch the machine as soon as it was in full flight.

After their four successive flights on that historic day, the Wrights knew that only practice was needed to go much farther before landing. Why not, as soon as they had eaten their lunch, fly the four miles up to the Kitty Hawk Weather Station where Mr. Dosher, the telegraph operator, was? They might as well use up the rest of the three pints of gasoline in the tank. But while they were standing there talking, a gust of wind struck the machine and turned it over.

John T. Daniels, of the Kill Devil Coast Guard station, tried to hold the machine, but it turned over and over, and he was badly bruised; he was the first airplane casualty. The machine was too badly damaged for any more flights that year. Indeed, they never did fly that machine again.]

5. The Wright brothers' first camp set up for assembling and testing gliders, just outside of Kitty Hawk, Dare County, North Carolina, September or (probably) October 1900.

6. A closer view of the tent at the Kitty Hawk camp, October 1900. The man in front of the tent is Orville, who did all of the cooking.

7. The first glider assembled at Kitty Hawk, 1900, here shown being flown as a kite. It had an elevator (the structure extending to the left) but no rudder. Turns were made solely by twisting or "warping" the wings. A structure on the opposite side of the plane—the rear—that first bore twin vertical fixed vanes and later a rudder was added much later, in 1902.

8

9

8. Beginning in late July 1901, the Wrights began experiments with an improved glider, their second model. By now they had moved to a more suitable location at the Kill Devil Hills, a few miles south of Kitty Hawk.

9. The underside of the 1901 glider, Orville standing at the left.

10. The Kill Devil Hills camp, early August 1901. Seated on a cot in the shed are, from the left, Octave Chanute, upon whose voluminous knowledge of previous attempts at flight the Wright brothers drew and who was a constant source of encouragement; Orville; and E. C. Huffaker, an associate of Chanute's with whom Chanute was building a glider of their own. Wilbur is standing at the right. This was the first and last time the brothers went to the Kitty Hawk area in midsummer. They found the heat too fierce and the mosquitoes and sand fleas intolerable.

11

11. The 1901 glider being launched by Dan Tate, a local resident (left), and Huffaker. The face of whichever Wright is in the glider is obscured by the front elevator.

12. Wilbur flying the 1901 glider.

13. Wilbur in the 1901 glider at the end of a glide.

12

13

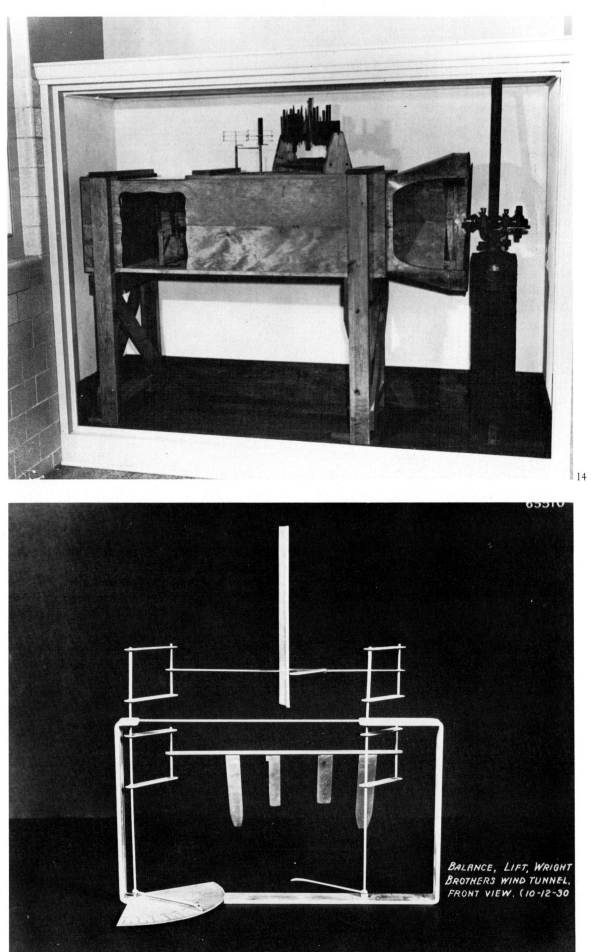

14

65510

BALANCE, LIFT, WRIGHT
BROTHERS WIND TUNNEL.
FRONT VIEW. (10-12-30

Camp.

14. Toward the end of August 1901 the Wrights returned to Dayton and built the world's first wind tunnel to test the aerodynamic properties of wing surfaces. Presumed lost, the tunnel was reconstructed by the U.S. Army Air Corps for exhibition at the restored bicycle shop at Greenfield Village. The restored tunnel is the one seen in this photograph, taken 1939. (The original wind tunnel, with testing apparatus, was recovered near the end of Orville's life.)

15. Replica of a testing apparatus that had been built for use with the original 1901 wind tunnel. (Photograph taken 1939.)

16. View of the camp near the Kill Devil Hills, 1902, during a rainy period. The following year the tent was replaced by a second shed. The handwriting is apparently that of Bishop Milton Wright.

17. A rare view of the interior of the camp shed upon the Wright brothers' arrival in the late summer of 1902. The partly disassembled 1901 glider is at the right. The man standing at the rear is Wilbur.

18. The camp kitchen, 1902.

19. The 1902 glider being flown as a kite. For the first time, the brothers added a structure in the rear (at right in the photograph) with twin vertical fixed vanes.

20. Wilbur in the 1902 glider.

21. The 1902 glider after modification in October. The fixed double vanes were replaced by a single adjustable rudder. Sitting on the ground, from the left, are Chanute; Orville; Wilbur; A. M. Herring, an associate of Chanute's; George Spratt, a doctor who had been invited at Chanute's urging; and Dan Tate. (Photograph taken October 10, 1902.)

22. Octave Chanute's triple-wing glider being tested, October 1902, at Kill Devil Hills. This glider did not have any equivalent of the revolutionary system of wing control that the Wrights had invented. (Chanute's visit to the Wrights' camp lasted from October 5 to 14, 1902.)

23. The modified 1902 glider being launched, October 10. From the left: Wilbur, Orville, Dan Tate.

24. The 1902 glider after release.

25. The 1902 glider in flight, Wilbur aboard.

24.

25

26. The 1902 glider turning to the left.

27. The 1902 glider turning to the right. "Wing warping" is clearly evident in this rear view. The position of the wings and rudder are the opposite of what might be expected. This indicates that the turn has already begun and the controls have been adjusted to compensate for the tendency toward excessive tilt in the direction of the lower wing.

28. The 1902 glider in flight. The camp shed may be seen in the distance.

29. The brothers' sleeping quarters in one of the camp sheds, 1903.

30. The 1902 glider with the camp in the distance, October 21, 1903. While they were assembling the new powered machine they had brought to Kill Devil Hills, the Wrights made a number of flights in the glider of the previous year, now further modified with a rudder similar to the one they would use on the powered machine. The second building had been erected shortly before this time. The puddles of water near the shed are a result of the severe storms that this part of the country had recently experienced. The ocean can be dimly discerned near the horizon. This photograph appeared with the Wrights' *Century Magazine* article; the caption stated that the glider flights of this period "lasted from forty-five seconds to a minute and ten seconds."

31. The newly assembled Flyer (for a long time the Wrights named each of their powered airplanes "Flyer," a sort of combined generic and proper name), soon to be the world's first successful man-carrying heavier-than-air flying machine, at the Wrights' camp, late 1903. The man is (apparently) Wilbur.

32. A front view of the Flyer. The droop in the wings seemed right for the terrain of the Kill Devil Hills but proved aerodynamically unsound for flying elsewhere. The droop did not appear in the wings of any Wright machine after early 1905.

33. The original motor used to power the 1903 Flyer. (Photograph taken at the bicycle shop on January 10, 1928, when the motor was being restored for exhibition with the Flyer at the Science Museum, London.)

34. Another view of the motor. This four-cylinder internal-combustion engine, specially designed and built by the Wrights for their airplane, developed over 12 hp, fifty percent more power than they had calculated was necessary to lift their Flyer off the ground.

33

34

35. Wilbur in the grounded Flyer after the first—unsuccessful—attempt at flight, December 14, 1903. It took a few days to repair the damage before Orville, whose turn it now was, could attempt another flight, this time meeting success.

36. Success at last! Possibly the most famous aviation picture of all time, this photograph of the 1903 Flyer in the air, with Orville at the controls, was taken at 10:35 A.M., December 17, 1903, by John T. Daniels of the Kill Devil Life Saving Station, acting under Orville's instructions. Wilbur stands at the right. This 12-second flight into a 27-mph headwind was the first of four successful flights that day. The plane as shown in this photograph would fly about another hundred feet (total of 120 feet) at a maximum altitude of about ten feet before coming to rest. Besides Daniels, four other local residents witnessed this first truly successful flight in history.

After the First Flights

by ORVILLE WRIGHT

THESE FIRST FLIGHTS having demonstrated the possibility of man flight with a motor, after our return to Dayton we decided to build another machine with stronger landing gear and to continue the experiments, to acquire more skill in the handling of the machine, the lack of which had terminated each of the four flights at Kitty Hawk on December 17, 1903.

We built another machine during the winter and spring of 1904, almost exactly like the one used at Kitty Hawk, excepting that most of the parts were built heavier and stronger. A new motor was installed which furnished 16 horsepower, as compared with 12 or 13 horsepower of 1903.

The field upon which the flights were made in 1904 [Huffman pasture] lay at the intersection of the main road between Dayton and Springfield, and the road running to Yellow Springs, Ohio. The electric line between Dayton and Springfield also ran along one side of the field.

During the year 1904, 105 flights or attempted flights were made; the longest of these were two having each a duration of over five minutes and each covering a course of three complete circles.

The weight of this 1904 machine was 925 pounds (including the weight of the operator, about 145 pounds, and 90 pounds of steel bars which were also carried).[1] The speed of the machine varied from 32 to 38 miles an hour. As it was not possible to start this machine from the short monorail which we used, except in winds of 11 miles and over, late in the year we began using a falling weight to assist in launching.

The two [longer] flights referred to were made on the 9th of November and the 1st of December, 1904. The first had a duration of five minutes four seconds, the second five minutes eight seconds. The first flight covered almost four rounds and the second was about the same length. The machine at this time had approximately a speed of 38 miles per hour, so that the circuits were approximately three quarters of a mile each.

On the 23d of May, 1905, we began assembling a new machine in the building on the Huffman

---

[1]The 1903 machine weighed 750 pounds with operator.

prairie. This 1905 machine was similar to that of 1904, but the curvature of the ribs was one-twentieth instead of one-twenty-fifth to one-thirtieth of the chord, as was the curvature of the 1904 rib at the end of the season. The controls of the 1905 machine were operated in a slightly different manner from those of the 1903 machine. The vertical rear rudder was not connected up . . . to automatically operate in conjunction with the wing warping, but instead was coupled up to a lever, so that it could be operated either independently of the warping or in conjunction therewith. It was operated in this manner in a few of the flights in 1904, but not in many of that year.

In addition to the change in the method of operating the rear vertical rudder, another modification in the system of control was used in the early flights of 1905. This was the addition of two vertical fixed vanes, forward of the main planes and attached to the front elevator framing. By the use of these fixed forward vanes an effect was secured just the opposite of that when the vanes are placed in the rear of the main planes. In other words, when the machine began sliding sidewise, due to one wing being slightly lower than the other, a pressure was created on that side of the vanes which was toward the low wing, and as a result, the speed of the lower wing was increased and that of the upper wing decreased. This was an effect similar to that secured from the movable rear rudder. The effect of these forward fixed vanes is secured in machines today from the forward vertical sides of the fuselage. At the beginning of the experiments of 1905 the wings had a slight droop, but later this was changed so that the wings had a dihedral angle at the center but were made straight at the tips.

During the year 1905, 50 flights were made, having a total duration of over 216 minutes in the air. Between September 26 and October 5, 1905, 6 flights were made, ranging in duration from 17 minutes 15 seconds, to 38 minutes 3 seconds.

Immediately upon the completion of our experiments in 1905, we wrote a letter to Captain Ferber in France, telling him of what we had accomplished during the year. A month later letters were sent to the secretary of the Aéro Club of France, to Patrick Alexander, a member of the Aeronautical Society of Great Britain, and to Carl Dientsbach, correspondent for the *Illustrierte Aeronautische Mitteilungen*, of Strassburg, Germany. The letters [to] Ferber and to the secretary of the Aéro Club of France were published in a number of the daily papers of Paris, as well as in *l'Aérophile*, and created a furore in aeronautical circles abroad. We also sent, a short time after this, a letter to the Aero Club of America, which had just then been founded.

[*In the spring of 1903, the Wrights' friend Chanute, on a visit to his native Paris, had revealed in a lecture and in articles for scientific magazines details of the Wrights' 1902 glider, with photographs and drawings. The French immediately seized upon this information and began experiments that led to successful European aviation. They could not have succeeded without knowledge of the wing design and method of control that the Wrights had learned by research and experiment. All aviation, whether American or European, stems from the Wrights.*]

37. In 1904 the Wrights built a new Flyer at their new center of operations, a pasture owned by Dayton banker Torrence Huffman, at Simms Station, eight miles east of Dayton. Orville and Wilbur are seen here with their new machine on the field, often known as Huffman Prairie, May 1904.

38. The flight of November 16, 1904, at Simms Station. The row of trees marks the route of the Dayton-Springfield electric interurban railroad. Photographs in the *Century Magazine* article pictured this flight as well as that of November 9, in which, according to a caption, "the machine described almost four complete circles, covering a distance of three miles in five minutes and four seconds."

39. The flight of September 29, 1905, Simms Station. Orville is at the controls. This Flyer is a new one, which, after some modifications made about this time, became the first fully practical flying machine in history. Note the extended outrigger attaching the front elevators to the body of the plane.

40. The flight of September 29, 1905: front view. This flight covered twelve miles. On October 4, Orville flew over twenty miles in 33 minutes, 17 seconds. Photographs of the latter flight were included with the original *Century Magazine* article. (The longest flight of the year was on October 5: over 24 miles in 39 minutes, 24 seconds.)

After Kitty Hawk: A Brief Résumé ————

by FRED C. KELLY

EVEN AFTER THE Wrights had brought the airplane to the stage of development for practical use, the stupendous thing they had done still seemed too incredible to be taken seriously, and they had not yet won much recognition. Newspapers in their own city of Dayton did not yet quite know who they were or what it was they had invented. The Dayton *Herald* of Thursday, March 21, 1907, three years and three months after the first flights, referred to them as "inventors of the airship," and Orville's name was given as "Oliver."

The Wrights did no flying during 1906 or 1907 but were building six or seven machines, and also giving much attention to the question of what to do with the airplane. As early as 1905 they began to receive inquiries from abroad and to receive overtures from representatives of foreign governments; but they wanted the United States Government to have first opportunity not only to use the machine for any military need, but also to control all rights in the invention for the entire world. They thought observations from scouting planes could prevent surprise attacks by an enemy. They saw, too, that it would be possible to drop bombs on enemy territory. And they hoped no government would want to risk starting a war and subjecting its people to the kind of devastation the airplane could inflict. One thing they particularly believed might prevent war was the opportunity the airplane provided promptly to drop bombs on buildings occupied by the highest government officials or rulers of the country that declared war. They hoped their invention would thus make war so inadvisable that no government would dare to start one.

With all this in mind, as early as January, 1905, they wrote to their representative in Congress, Mr. Nevin, asking him to find out if the United States War Department would be interested in the invention, explaining that "the numerous flights in straight lines, in circles, and over S-shaped courses, in calms and in winds, have made it quite certain that flying has been brought to a point where it can be made of great practical use."

The Congressman forwarded the letter to the War Department.

In reply, a Major General of the General Staff, who was President of the Board of Ordnance and Fortification, sent a silly letter. "The Board has found it necessary," the letter said, "to decline to make allotments for the experimental development of devices for mechanical flight," and it added that before the Board could consider suggestions with that object in view, *the device must have been brought to the stage of practical operation*, without expense to the United States.

"It appears from the letter of Messrs. Wilbur and Orville Wright," the perspicacious Major General went on to say, "that their machine *has not yet been brought to the stage of practical operation.*" (Italics added.)

The Wrights, remember, had not even hinted at wanting money for experimental work and had explained in detail that their machine had already reached the stage of practical operation.

Naturally, the Wrights were disinclined to expose themselves to further rebuffs from the War Department but, urged on by their friend Chanute, nine months later, in October, 1905, they made another offer of their machine to the Government, pointing out that the Government would not need to accept any contract until after the machine had made a trial performance of at least twenty-five miles at a speed of not less than thirty miles an hour.

This time another Major General signed the reply, but part of it was almost word for word the same as the previous one. The Government would not be interested *until after the machine had been brought to the stage of practical operation!* The letter said that, before considering a contract, the Government would want to see drawings and descriptions, to make possible a definite conclusion as to the machine's practicability.

In short, the Ordnance Board would have to study drawings to determine if the airplane the Wrights had been flying *could* fly!

The Wrights curbed their irritation and replied to the letter, stating once again that they were not asking financial assistance and proposed to sell the results of experiments completed at their own expense. To which the Board of Ordnance replied that they did not care to take any further action on the subject *until a machine is produced which by actual operation is shown to be able to produce horizontal flight and to carry an operator.*

There wasn't much the Wrights could do in the face of such nonsense, and they began dickering with foreign governments, while leaving the door open for negotiations with the United States Government. It was not until February 8, 1908, that the Signal Corps of the United States War Department made a contract with the Wrights for an airplane. Only three weeks later the Wrights closed a contract with a Frenchman to form a syndicate for the rights to manufacture, sell, or license the use of the Wright machine in France.

Wilbur and Orville revamped their 1905 machine, to permit the pilot to sit upright instead of lying prone, and to carry a passenger. In May, 1908, they took the machine to Kitty Hawk to get practice for demonstrations they would make, for the United States Government, near Washington, and for the French company in France. (That 1905 machine, in its original form, has been restored and is now in a Dayton museum.)

Orville met with a serious accident during his demonstrations at Fort Myer, near Washington, and the United States Government contract was not completed until July 30, 1909, when he finished his series of test flights. He then went to Germany to make flights required in the formation of a German Wright company. Meanwhile Wilbur had received many prizes and awards for his flights in France, where he also taught a number of Frenchmen to fly. The Wrights sold a machine in Italy, and Wilbur trained fliers there. (A British Wright company was not formed until 1913.)

While Orville was making sensational flights in Germany, Wilbur, in America, was doing his share to glorify the brotherly partnership. On September 29, as part of the Hudson-Fulton Celebration, he made spectacular flights seen by millions of people. Two of these were over Governors Island; and another was from Governors Island around the Statue of Liberty and back again. Then, on October 4, Wilbur flew twenty-one miles from Governors Island up the Hudson River beyond Grant's Tomb and back to the starting point, one of the most daring flights yet made.

Almost immediately after his flights for the Hudson-Fulton Celebration, Wilbur went to College Park, Maryland, near Washington, to train as pilots two Army Signal Corps officers, as provided for in the Government contract.

That eventful year, 1909, also saw the organization, in November, of The Wright Company in the United States, with Wilbur Wright as president. The company opened a flying school, first near Montgomery, Alabama, and then at Huffman field, eight miles from Dayton, where the practice flights during 1904-05 had been made. It was here that Lieutenant "Hap" Arnold, later General Arnold, head of all Army Air Forces and Assistant Chief of Staff for Air in World War II, learned to fly. On May 25, 1910, Wilbur and Orville flew together, with Orville piloting, the only occasion when they risked being in the air at the same time. Later that same day Orville took his father, aged eighty-two, for his first airplane ride. They flew at about 350 feet. His father wanted to go higher.

New as aviation business was, it was profitable almost from the start. The greater part of The Wright Company's income at first came from public exhibitions of flying. Millions of people had not yet seen a machine in the air. A Wright pilot, Brookins, in 1910, made the first long, cross-country flight, 185 miles, to Springfield, Illinois, from Chicago.

Orville Wright took time off in the autumn of 1911 to return to Kitty Hawk to do some experimenting with an automatic control device, and to make soaring flights with a glider. Because of the presence of newspapermen, he did not try the automatic control device. On October 24 he set a new soaring record of nine minutes forty-five seconds, which remained a world's record until exceeded, in Germany, ten years later.

Now that flying had become big business, the Wrights were plagued by the need of bringing suits against patent infringers. One of the most persistent infringers was Glenn H. Curtiss. The suit against Curtiss and The Herring-Curtiss Company was carried to the highest court it could be, where the Wrights won.

In France, too, there were many infringers and the French Wright Company brought suit. Among the infringers named there were Blériot, who won fame by being the first to fly across the English Channel; and Santos-Dumont, who, in 1906, was the first to fly in Europe. No claim for damages was made against Santos-Dumont, and his name was dropped, since he flew only for sport and showed no disposition to try to make money from aviation. The Wrights won every one of their patent suits that was ever adjudicated.

In 1912 Wilbur Wright contracted typhoid fever and after lingering for three weeks died, on May 30. Orville succeeded him as president of The Wright Company.

The Wrights had not been happy as businessmen and had been looking forward to the time when they could devote themselves to scientific research. Now, with Wilbur gone, Orville found business details even less congenial. Moreover, he became annoyed over what he saw going on within The Wright Company. The New Yorkers who had organized the company were Tammany men, and Orville believed they wanted to use the company for political purposes. For example, they wished to employ an attorney, to be stationed in Washington; and the chief reason for his selection, it appeared, was that he was known to be a close friend of President Wilson, with easy access to the White House.

Orville would have liked to retire from the company, but could not do so, for he was under contract to remain with it for a term of years. So, he took the only alternative. When his associates complained that he didn't seem willing to "play ball," he promptly suggested that he would be glad to buy them all out, paying them enough, including dividends they had received, to give them a profit on their original investment of one hundred per cent. This deal was finally made. Orville bought out all the other stockholders with the exception of his friend Robert J. Collier. To carry out his part, Orville had to borrow money, the first time he had ever done so in connection with aviation. However, he was not long in debt. Only a few months later, in 1915, he resold the company to eastern capitalists at a profit which represented the greatest return he had received from the invention of the airplane.

Later, the Wright and the Curtiss companies were merged.

Orville Wright had received in 1913 the Aero Club of America Trophy (now called the Robert J. Collier trophy) for his invention of an automatic stabilizer. With other ideas he wished to work on, he built in 1916 an office and workshop at 15 N. Broadway, in Dayton, that was to be his headquarters for the rest of his life. There, with a wind tunnel a little larger than the one he and Wilbur had used, he made studies of different methods of wind-tunnel testing that had come into use. He was still at this work when the

United States entered the First World War and Dayton men formed the Dayton Wright Company to build Liberty motors and the American version of the DH-4 airplane. Orville became the director of engineering and devoted himself to work on the De Havilland machine. About one thousand of the machines had been delivered by the Dayton company when the Armistice of 1918 ended the war.

Orville continued to carry on experiments. One of his later inventions was the so-called split wing-flap, for use in slowing down a machine for landings. All the rest of his life he was a member of the National Advisory Committee for Aeronautics.

A thing that caused Orville Wright much annoyance during many years, starting in 1914, was a controversy with the Smithsonian Institution, which had published misstatements that if accepted would have cast doubt upon the priority of the Wrights as inventors of the airplane. Because of these misstatements and the unwillingness of the Smithsonian for a long time to admit its error, Orville did not wish to entrust the original Wright 1903 plane to the National Museum, administered by the Smithsonian, and in 1928 he lent the machine to the Science Museum at South Kensington, near London, England.* There it was on exhibition for twenty years. But in October, 1942, the controversy with the Smithsonian was amicably settled. The Institution publicly withdrew its previous misstatements and offered full apology. Orville then asked for the return of the original plane from England. Because of war conditions it could not be shipped across the Atlantic at that time; but after Orville's death, which occurred on January 30, 1948, the machine was brought back and deposited by the Wright executors in the National Air Museum. It was formally installed there on December 17, 1948, the forty-fifth anniversary of the first flights.

The exhibition label on the machine includes the following:

THE ORIGINAL WRIGHT BROTHERS AEROPLANE
THE WORLD'S FIRST
POWER-DRIVEN HEAVIER-THAN-AIR MACHINE
IN WHICH MAN

---

*[Actually *in* London.—1988 note.]

MADE FREE, CONTROLLED, AND SUSTAINED
FLIGHT
INVENTED AND BUILT BY WILBUR AND
ORVILLE WRIGHT
FLOWN BY THEM AT KITTY HAWK, NORTH
CAROLINA
DECEMBER 17, 1903
BY ORIGINAL, SCIENTIFIC RESEARCH THE
WRIGHT BROTHERS
DISCOVERED THE PRINCIPLES OF HUMAN
FLIGHT
AS INVENTORS, BUILDERS, AND FLYERS
THEY FURTHER DEVELOPED THE AEROPLANE,
TAUGHT MAN TO
FLY, AND OPENED THE ERA OF AVIATION

Orville Wright was in his seventy-seventh year at the end, but in his later years he continued to show a boyish quality, with a fondness for pranks. He could turn his inventiveness to playful purposes. Once he prepared a turkey in a special way for a family dinner on Thanksgiving Day. Nearly all his nieces and nephews preferred dark meat, and this time they were surprised that, as Uncle Orv carved, the supply never gave out. One of them remarked, "This is good turkey, but it tastes a little like duck." Then Orville turned the platter around to show that the turkey was only a façade. Most of the dark meat *was* duck.

Contrary to the common impression that he was taciturn and reticent, Orville Wright loved to talk. When with anyone to whom he could speak frankly, he would sit up far into the night; and there is no record of any of his friends ever seeing him yawn. I talked with him frequently during a third of a century; and, whenever I went to his home in the evening, I promised myself that I would not keep him up too late, but would leave not later than ten o'clock. Almost never, however, did I get away before one o'clock in the morning. Around midnight Orville would just be getting warmed up to something he wanted to discuss.

One night I asked him when it was, during the early attempts to fly, that he and Wilbur felt most discouraged. His reply seemed so interesting that as soon as possible I made full notes of it.

"When we discovered in 1901 that tables of air pressures prepared by our predecessors were not accurate or dependable, that was discouraging, in a way, and disappointing. For it meant that instead of starting from where others had left off, as we had expected to do, we must start from scratch. But on the other hand the fact that these data, which others had considered accurate, now turned out to be inaccurate was interesting. One gets a certain thrill from discovering something others have not known. From one way of looking at it, you might even have called it encouraging, that the data others had used could not be relied upon. It suggested that maybe the reason others had failed to fly was not because the thing couldn't be done."

Once I asked him what his feeling was about the use of the airplane as an instrument of wholesale destruction and human slaughter. Did he ever wish he had never invented it?

"No," he replied promptly. "I don't have any regrets about my part in the invention of the airplane, though no one could deplore more than I do the destruction it has caused. I feel about the airplane much as I do in regard to fire. That is, I regret all the terrible damage caused by fire. But I think it is good for the human race that someone discovered how to start fires and that it is possible to put fire to thousands of important uses."

"How much did you and Wilbur foresee of the use of the airplane for war purposes?"

"At the time we first flew our power plane we were not thinking of any practical uses at all. We just wanted to show that it was possible to fly. Even for some time afterward we didn't suppose it would ever be possible to fly or make landings at night."

I recall one other question, about when he got the biggest "kick" out of the invention. Was it when the machine took off in the first flight ever made?

"No," Orville said, "I got more thrill out of flying before I had ever been in the air at all—while lying in bed thinking how exciting it would be to fly."

41

43

42

41. When the Wrights returned to Kill Devil Hills in April 1908, they found that the harsh weather of the region had left their sheds in ruins. The remains of the 1902 glider may be seen in and around the shed on the left. When this photograph was taken, the building at the right had already been reconstructed.

42. In May 1908, Wilbur went to France to prepare for a series of demonstrations called for by an agreement with a syndicate of French businessmen. The demonstrations began on August 8 at the Hunaudières racecourse near Le Mans, with a machine that had been shipped to Europe for such a purpose and assembled in France under Wilbur's supervision. (Orville, meanwhile, was preparing a similar series of demonstrations for the U.S. Army, near Washington, D.C.) Wilbur is seen here at the controls of the Flyer at Hunaudières. Notice that the pilot could now sit upright and space has been made for a passenger.

43. The Flyer at takeoff, Hunaudières, August 1908.

44

44. Spectators view Wilbur in flight, Hunaudières, August 1908. These were the first public airplane demonstrations of any consequence and convinced many skeptics of the feasibility of controlled heavier-than-air flight.

45. Wilbur directs a crew of workmen removing the left wing of his Flyer, damaged at the end of the last flight of August 13 at Hunaudières.

46. On August 20, 1908, Orville, who had remained in the United States, brought a new Flyer to Fort Myer, Virginia, just across the Potomac River from Washington, D.C., to demonstrate it to the U.S. Army Signal Corps in fulfillment of a government contract effected earlier that year. In this photograph, dating from that time, the partly disassembled Flyer is being hauled to the takeoff site on a military supply wagon. Orville, wearing a straw hat, stands on the running board of the automobile.

47

47. Orville in flight over Fort Myer, September 1908. As is evident in this photograph, the testing ground was relatively small. To assist in achieving rapid takeoff in so confined a space, a special launching derrick with a falling weight was used (dimly visible in the background, to right of center); this had been devised by the Wrights at the Huffman field in 1904 and was also being used by Wilbur in his European demonstrations.

48. Before the last flight at Fort Myer, September 17, 1908. Orville's passenger was 26-year-old Lt. Thomas E. Selfridge, who had himself recently been involved in aviation experiments. Although Selfridge's expression is serious, almost grim, he could not have known that he would be dead in a few hours. After a few minutes in the air, a flaw in a propeller caused a chain reaction that sent the plane into a dive from which Orville could not recover. Selfridge's injuries were fatal—his was the first airplane-passenger death in history—and Orville was very seriously hurt.

49. Fort Myer, September 17, 1908. The Flyer, shortly after its crash landing. The men under the wing are attempting to remove Orville from the wreckage; the fatally injured Lt. Selfridge lies at the right, just out of sight of the camera.

48

49

50

50. Orville with Hart O. Berg, the Wrights' agent in non-English-speaking European countries, photographed in Paris, January 1909. Orville displays a smile rarely captured in photographs of him; his cane reminds us that he was still recovering from his recent accident. Orville was in the French capital with his sister Katharine; their brother Wilbur, having just completed his series of flying demonstrations at Le Mans, came up to join them.

51. In mid-January 1909, Wilbur resumed his flying demonstrations, this time at Pau, at the edge of the Pyrenees in southwest France, where the climate was warmer than at Le Mans. At Pau he was visited by such dignitaries as King Edward VII of England and King Alfonso XIII of Spain. The horse-drawn carriages in the photograph contrast startlingly with the newfangled flying machine overhead. Wilbur's passenger is his French pupil Paul Tissandier.

52. At Pau, on February 15, 1909, Katharine Wright flew for the first time. Orville stands at the left.

51

52

‹ 55

53. Wilbur tests the wind speed with an anemometer, Pau, 1909.

54. King Alfonso XIII of Spain, seated aboard the Flyer in February 1909, asks Wilbur a question.

55. Another of Wilbur's flights at Pau, this time with Capt. Paul N. Lucas-Girardville, one of Wilbur's other French pilots-in-training. Wilbur also made a series of flights near Rome in the second half of April 1909, before returning to the United States.

56. Orville resumed his test flights for the U.S. Army at Fort Myer at the end of June 1909. This time Wilbur was also present. In this photograph, military men seated on the launching derrick are watching Orville in flight (probably the month is July, as only a very few flights at a very low altitude were made in June). The two men in shirtsleeves with their backs to the camera are Wilbur (left) and Charles E. Taylor, the Wrights' chief mechanic.

57. The Flyer being placed on the launching track at Fort Myer, 1909. Orville is standing between the skids.

58. Military personnel attach the launching cable to the Flyer, Fort Myer, 1909. On August 2, after successful testing, the Wright brothers' Flyer was formally purchased by the U.S. government.

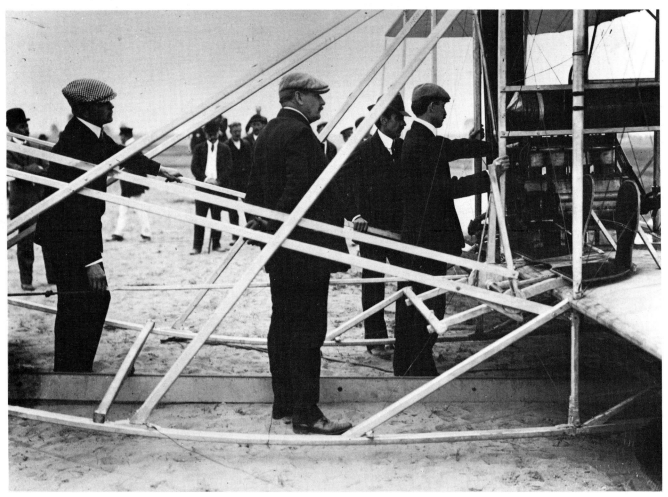

59. Immediately after the successful Fort Myer demonstrations, Orville returned to Europe to demonstrate the Flyer in Germany, where he remained until the middle of October 1909. Here he is seen adjusting the motor before a group of interested spectators at Tempelhof field, Berlin.

60. A group of soldiers views one of Orville's flights.

61. Another flight at Tempelhof field; a lone soldier on horseback watches from below.

62

62. Katharine and Orville Wright with German aristocracy at Tempelhof field.

63. Orville with German Crown Prince Friedrich Wilhelm and Hart O. Berg at Tempelhof field. A few weeks later the Crown Prince became the first member of any royal family to fly in an airplane.

Die vom

„BERLINER LOKAL-ANZEIGER"
veranstalteten Flugvorführungen ══
ORVILLE WRIGHTS
in Berlin.

Orville Wright

Kronprinz

Originalaufnahme 1909.

64. While Orville was flying in Germany, Wilbur, back in the United States, gave a spectacular series of demonstrations at the Hudson-Fulton Exhibition in New York, on September 29 and October 4, 1909. Here he is flying low over Governors Island in New York harbor, the base of his operations. The dark shape under the plane is a specially sealed canoe that Wilbur had hoped would keep the plane afloat should an emergency force it into the water (the canoe fortunately never had to be tested). On September 29 Wilbur took the Flyer in a circuit around the Statue of Liberty.

65. Wilbur heading southeast over the Hudson River on the return leg of a 21-mile flight over water to Grant's Tomb (in upper Manhattan), October 4, 1909. This was one of the longest and most daring flights yet undertaken by anyone. The skyline of lower Manhattan, including the new Singer Building (with the spire), is visible at the right. It is often assumed that Wilbur Wright was the first to fly an airplane in New York City. Actually the visiting French aviator Henri Farman had flown his Voisin biplane on July 31, 1908, at the Brighton Beach Race Track in Brooklyn, well within New York City limits. Nevertheless, Wilbur's flights were far more extensive and technically advanced and were the first to be observed by most New Yorkers.

66. Another view of Wilbur over Governors Island. The Manhattan skyline to the north is dimly visible past the wings; Castle Williams (built 1807-11) stands at the left. Note the small American flag tied to the right side of the front elevator.

67

68

67. Wilbur Wright in front of his plane at the Hudson-Fulton Exhibition, October 4, 1909. From the left: Captain Halstead Dovey; the Honorable James M. Beck, chairman of aeronautical activities; Charles E. Taylor; Wilbur; and William J. Hammer.

68. Early in 1910, the Wrights, through their newly founded Wright Company, opened a flying school near Montgomery, Alabama, where the climate was suitable for winter aviation. Orville was the instructor; his first pupil was Walter Brookins, whom he had known in Dayton since the latter was a child. Brookins went on to become Orville's assistant instructor and trained several other pilots. This photograph of Orville, Brookins, and four pilots-in-training was taken in the hangar at the Montgomery school in the spring of 1910. From the left: A. L. (Arthur L.) Welsh, Spencer C. Crane, Orville, Walter Brookins, James Davis, Arch Hoxsey. Most of these men soon became well-known aviators; most also died young in the practice of what was, especially in those early days, an extremely hazardous occupation.

69. Hoxsey, Brookins, and Crane wheeling a Flyer out of the hangar at the Montgomery flying school, spring 1910.

GENERAL ASSEMBLY DEPARTMENT

70. Another branch of the Wrights' school was opened at the Huffman field, Simms Station, mid-1910, where pilots could be trained during the warmer months. Here the photographer captured Orville with five of his student pilots. From the left: Duval La Chapelle, A. L. Welsh, Orville, James Davis, Ralph Johnstone, and Frank Coffyn.

71. A Model B Flyer being constructed in the General Assembly Department of the Wright Company factory in Dayton, 1911. The Wrights had begun to manufacture planes in quantity in 1910. The first plane made, the Model B, had much the same basic structure as the Model A, the plane sold to the Army the previous year; but there were a few significant changes. Most fundamental was the transfer of the elevator from the front to the rear structure that held the rudder. Two fixed flaps of cloth were added to what remained of the forward structure; these provided stability in turns. For the first time also, wheels were added to the undercarriage. A number of smaller versions of this plane— single-seat models for racing and the like—were also manufactured around this time.

72. The Model B1 Flyer, fitted with pontoons for testing by the Navy, San Diego Bay, California, 1912.

73

74

75

73. On June 22, 1927, a few weeks after his famous solo trans-Atlantic flight, Charles A. Lindbergh (second from right in the photograph) paid Orville (wearing the straw hat) a visit in Dayton. Between them in the photograph stands Maj. John F. Curry of the Army Air Corps. Since the death of Wilbur on May 30, 1912, Orville had continued their experimental work in aircraft design, but he had not himself flown as a pilot since 1918.

74. A controversy with the Smithsonian Institution led Orville to loan the original Flyer of 1903 to the Science Museum, London, in 1928. The occasion of this photograph, showing the Flyer (with a dummy Wright brother as pilot!) on display at the museum, was a dinner on December 17 commemorating the twenty-fifth anniversary of the first flight.

75. Orville with Henry Ford at the Ford Museum, Greenfield Village, Dearborn, Michigan, June 26, 1937. Charles Taylor, who had been the Wrights' mechanic since before the days of the first Flyer, stands between Orville and Ford as they examine the diagram of a machine in the restored bicycle shop.

76. President Franklin D. Roosevelt with Orville in the president's car on an inspection tour of Wright Field, Dayton, October 12, 1940.

Appendix

The Wright Brothers' Aëroplane————————

by ORVILLE AND WILBUR WRIGHT

THE article which follows is the first popular account of their experiments prepared by the inventors. Their accounts heretofore have been brief statements of bare accomplishments, without explanation of the manner in which results were attained. The article will be found of special interest, in view of the fact that they have contracted to deliver to the United States Government a complete machine, the trials of which are expected to take place about the time of the appearance of this number of THE CENTURY.—THE EDITOR [OF THE CENTURY].

THOUGH THE SUBJECT of aërial navigation is generally considered new, it has occupied the minds of men more or less from the earliest ages. Our personal interest in it dates from our childhood days. Late in the autumn of 1878, our father came into the house one evening with some object partly concealed in his hands, and before we could see what it was, he tossed it into the air. Instead of falling to the floor, as we expected, it flew across the room till it struck the ceiling, where it fluttered awhile, and finally sank to the floor. It was a little toy, known to scientists as a "hélicoptère," but which we, with sublime disregard for science, at once dubbed a "bat." It was a light frame of cork and bamboo, covered with paper, which formed two screws, driven in opposite directions by rubber bands under torsion. A toy so delicate lasted only a short time in the hands of small boys, but its memory was abiding.

Several years later we began building these hélicoptères for ourselves, making each one larger than that preceding. But, to our astonishment, we found that the larger the "bat," the less it flew. We did not know that a machine having only twice the linear dimensions of another would require eight times the power. We finally became discouraged, and returned to kite-flying, a sport to which we had devoted so much attention that we were regarded as experts. But as we became older, we had to give up this fascinating sport as unbecoming to boys of our ages.

It was not till the news of the sad death of Lilienthal reached America in the summer of 1896 that we again gave more than passing attention to the subject of flying. We then studied with great interest Chanute's "Progress in Flying Machines," Langley's "Experiments in Aërodynamics," the "Aëronautical Annuals" of 1905, 1906, and 1907, and several pamphlets published by the Smithsonian Institution, especially articles by Lilienthal and extracts from Mouillard's "Empire of the Air." The larger works gave us a good understanding of the nature of the flying problem, and the difficulties in past attempts to solve it, while Mouillard and Lilienthal, the great missionaries of the flying cause, infected us with their own unquenchable enthusiasm, and transformed idle curiosity into the active zeal of workers.

In the field of aviation there were two schools. The first, represented by such men as Professor Langley and Sir Hiram Maxim, gave chief attention to power flight; the second, represented by Lilienthal, Mouillard, and Chanute, to soaring flight. Our sympathies were with the latter school, partly from impatience at the wasteful extravagance of mounting delicate and costly machinery on wings which no one knew how to manage, and partly, no doubt, from the extraordinary charm and enthusiasm with which the apostles of soaring flight set forth the beauties of sailing through the air on fixed wings, deriving the motive power from the wind itself.

The balancing of a flyer may seem, at first thought, to be a very simple matter, yet almost every experimenter had found in this the one point which he could not satisfactorily master. Many different methods were tried. Some experimenters placed the center of gravity far below the wings, in the belief that the weight would naturally seek to remain at the lowest point. It was true, that, like the pendulum, it tended to seek the lowest point; but also, like the pendulum, it tended to oscillate in a manner destructive of all stability. A more satisfactory system, especially for lateral balance, was that of arranging the wings in the shape of a broad V, to form a dihedral angle, with the center low and the wing-tips elevated. In theory this was an automatic system, but in practice it had two serious defects: first, it tended to keep the machine oscillating; and, second, its usefulness was restricted to calm air.

In a slightly modified form the same system was applied to the fore-and-aft balance. The main

aëroplane was set at a positive angle, and a horizontal tail at a negative angle, while the center of gravity was placed far forward. As in the case of lateral control, there was a tendency to constant undulation, and the very forces which caused a restoration of balance in calms, caused a disturbance of the balance in winds. Notwithstanding the known limitations of this principle, it had been embodied in almost every prominent flying-machine which had been built.

After considering the practical effect of the dihedral principle, we reached the conclusion that a flyer founded upon it might be of interest from a scientific point of view, but could be of no value in a practical way. We therefore resolved to try a fundamentally different principle. We would arrange the machine so that it would not tend to right itself. We would make it as inert as possible to the effects of change of direction or speed, and thus reduce the effects of wind-gusts to a minimum. We would do this in the fore-and-aft stability by giving the aëroplanes a peculiar shape; and in the lateral balance, by arching the surfaces from tip to tip, just the reverse of what our predecessors had done. Then by some suitable contrivance, actuated by the operator, forces should be brought into play to regulate the balance.

Lilienthal and Chanute had guided and balanced their machines by shifting the weight of the operator's body. But this method seemed to us incapable of expansion to meet large conditions, because the weight to be moved and the distance of possible motion were limited, while the disturbing forces steadily increased, both with wing area and with wind velocity. In order to meet the needs of large machines, we wished to employ some system whereby the operator could vary at will the inclination of different parts of the wings, and thus obtain from the wind forces to restore the balance which the wind itself had disturbed. This could easily be done by using wings capable of being warped, and by supplementary adjustable surfaces in the shape of rudders. As the forces obtainable for control would necessarily increase in the same ratio as the disturbing forces, the method seemed capable of expansion to an almost unlimited extent. A happy device was discovered whereby the apparently rigid system of superposed surfaces, invented by Wenham, and improved by Stringfellow and

Chanute, could be warped in a most unexpected way, so that the aëroplanes could be presented on the right and left sides at different angles to the wind. This, with an adjustable, horizontal front rudder, formed the main feature of our first glider.

The period from 1885 to 1900 was one of unexampled activity in aëronautics, and for a time there was high hope that the age of flying was at hand. But Maxim, after spending $100,000, abandoned the work; the Ader machine, built at the expense of the French Government, was a failure; Lilienthal and Pilcher were killed in experiments; and Chanute and many others, from one cause or another, had relaxed their efforts, though it subsequently became known that Professor Langley was still secretly at work on a machine for the United States Government. The public, discouraged by the failures and tragedies just witnessed, considered flight beyond the reach of man, and classed its adherents with the inventors of perpetual motion.

We began our active experiments at the close of this period, in October, 1900, at Kitty Hawk, North Carolina. Our machine was designed to be flown as a kite, with a man on board, in winds of from fifteen to twenty miles an hour. But, upon trial, it was found that much stronger winds were required to lift it. Suitable winds not being plentiful, we found it necessary, in order to test the new balancing system, to fly the machine as a kite without a man on board, operating the levers through cords from the ground. This did not give the practice anticipated, but it inspired confidence in the new system of balance.

In the summer of 1901 we became personally acquainted with Mr. Chanute. When he learned that we were interested in flying as a sport, and not with any expectation of recovering the money we were expending on it, he gave us much encouragement. At our invitation, he spent several weeks with us at our camp at Kill Devil Hill, four miles south of Kitty Hawk, during our experiments of that and the two succeeding years. He also witnessed one flight of the power machine near Dayton, Ohio, in October, 1904.

The machine of 1901 was built with the shape of surface used by Lilienthal, curved from front to rear like the segment of a parabola, with a curvature $\frac{1}{12}$ the depth of its cord; but to make doubly sure that it would have sufficient lifting capacity when flown as a kite in fifteen- or twenty-mile winds, we increased the area from 165 square feet, used in 1900, to 308 square feet—a size much larger than Lilienthal, Pilcher, or Chanute had deemed safe. Upon trial, however, the lifting capacity again fell very far short of calculation, so that the idea of securing practice while flying as a kite, had to be abandoned. Mr. Chanute, who witnessed the experiments, told us that the trouble was not due to poor construction of the machine. We saw only one other explanation—that the tables of air-pressures in general use were incorrect.

We then turned to gliding—coasting down hill on the air—as the only method of getting the desired practice in balancing a machine. After a few minutes' practice we were able to make glides of over 300 feet, and in a few days were safely operating in twenty-seven-mile[1] winds. In these experiments we met with several unexpected phenomena. We found that, contrary to the teachings of the books, the center of pressure on a curved surface traveled backward when the surface was inclined, at small angles, more and more edgewise to the wind. We also discovered that in free flight, when the wing on one side of the machine was presented to the wind at a greater angle than the one on the other side, the wing with the greater angle descended, and the machine turned in a direction just the reverse of what we were led to expect when flying the machine as a kite. The larger angle gave more resistance to forward motion, and reduced the speed of the wing on that side. The decrease in speed more than counterbalanced the effect of the larger angle. The addition of a fixed vertical vane in the rear increased the trouble, and made the machine absolutely dangerous. It was some time before a remedy was discovered. This consisted of movable rudders working in conjunction with the twisting of the wings. The details of this arrangement are given in our patent specifications, published several years ago.

The experiments of 1901 were far from encouraging. Although Mr. Chanute assured us that, both in control and in weight carried per

---

[1]The gliding flights were all made against the wind. The difficulty in high winds is in maintaining balance, not in traveling against the wind.

horse-power, the results obtained were better than those of any of our predecessors, yet we saw that the calculations upon which all flying-machines had been based were unreliable, and that all were simply groping in the dark. Having set out with absolute faith in the existing scientific data, we were driven to doubt one thing after another, till finally, after two years of experiment, we cast it all aside, and decided to rely entirely upon our own investigations. Truth and error were everywhere so intimately mixed as to be undistinguishable. Nevertheless, the time expended in preliminary study of books was not misspent, for they gave us a good general understanding of the subject, and enabled us at the outset to avoid effort in many directions in which results would have been hopeless.

The standard for measurements of wind-pressures is the force produced by a current of air of one mile per hour velocity striking square against a plane of one square-foot area. The practical difficulties of obtaining an exact measurement of this force have been great. The measurements by different recognized authorities vary fifty per cent. When this simplest of measurements presents so great difficulties, what shall be said of the troubles encountered by those who attempt to find the pressure at each angle as the plane is inclined more and more edgewise to the wind? In the eighteenth century the French Academy prepared tables giving such information, and at a later date the Aëronautical Society of Great Britain made similar experiments. Many persons likewise published measurements and formulas; but the results were so discordant that Professor Langley undertook a new series of measurements, the results of which form the basis of his celebrated work, "Experiments in Aërodynamics." Yet a critical examination of the data upon which he based his conclusions as to the pressures at small angles shows results so various as to make many of his conclusions little better than guess-work.

To work intelligently, one needs to know the effects of a multitude of variations that could be incorporated in the surfaces of flying-machines. The pressures on squares are different from those on rectangles, circles, triangles, or ellipses; arched surfaces differ from planes, and vary among themselves according to the depth of curvature; true arcs differ from parabolas, and the latter differ among themselves; thick surfaces differ from thin, and surfaces thicker in one place than another vary in pressure when the positions of maximum thickness are different; some surfaces are most efficient at one angle, others at other angles. The shape of the edge also makes a difference, so that thousands of combinations are possible in so simple a thing as a wing.

We had taken up aëronautics merely as a sport. We reluctantly entered upon the scientific side of it. But we soon found the work so fascinating that we were drawn into it deeper and deeper. Two testing-machines were built, which we believed would avoid the errors to which the measurements of others had been subject. After making preliminary measurements on a great number of different-shaped surfaces, to secure a general understanding of the subject, we began systematic measurements of standard surfaces, so varied in design as to bring out the underlying causes of differences noted in their pressures. Measurements were tabulated on nearly fifty of these at all angles from zero to 45 degrees, at intervals of 2½ degrees. Measurements were also secured showing the effects on each other when surfaces are superposed, or when they follow one another.

Some strange results were obtained. One surface, with a heavy roll at the front edge, showed the same lift for all angles from 7½ to 45 degrees. A square plane, contrary to the measurements of all our predecessors, gave a greater pressure at 30 degrees than at 45 degrees. This seemed so anomalous that we were almost ready to doubt our own measurements, when a simple test was suggested. A weather-vane, with two planes attached to the pointer at an angle of 80 degrees with each other, was made. According to our tables, such a vane would be in unstable equilibrium when pointing directly into the wind; for if by chance the wind should happen to strike one plane at 39 degrees and the other at 41 degrees, the plane with the smaller angle would have the greater pressure, and the pointer would be turned still farther out of the course of the wind until the two vanes again secured equal pressures, which would be at approximately 30 and 50 degrees. But the vane performed in this very manner. Further corroboration of the tables was obtained in experiments with a new glider at Kill Devil Hill the next season.

In September and October, 1902, nearly one

thousand gliding flights were made, several of which covered distances of over 600 feet. Some, made against a wind of thirty-six miles an hour, gave proof of the effectiveness of the devices for control. With this machine, in the autumn of 1903, we made a number of flights in which we remained in the air for over a minute, often soaring for a considerable time in one spot, without any descent at all. Little wonder that our unscientific assistant should think the only thing needed to keep it indefinitely in the air would be a coat of feathers to make it light!

With accurate data for making calculations, and a system of balance effective in winds as well as in calms, we were now in a position, we thought, to build a successful power-flyer. The first designs provided for a total weight of 600 pounds, including the operator and an eight horse-power motor. But, upon completion, the motor gave more power than had been estimated, and this allowed 150 pounds to be added for strengthening the wings and other parts.

Our tables made the designing of the wings an easy matter; and as screw-propellers are simply wings traveling in a spiral course, we anticipated no trouble from this source. We had thought of getting the theory of the screw-propeller from the marine engineers, and then, by applying our tables of air-pressures to their formulas of designing air-propellers suitable for our purpose. But so far as we could learn, the marine engineers possessed only empirical formulas, and the exact action of the screw-propeller, after a century of use, was still very obscure. As we were not in a position to undertake a long series of practical experiments to discover a propeller suitable for our machine, it seemed necessary to obtain such a thorough understanding of the theory of its reactions as would enable us to design them from calculation alone. What at first seemed a simple problem became more complex the longer we studied it. With the machine moving forward, the air flying backward, the propellers turning sidewise, and nothing standing still, it seemed impossible to find a starting-point from which to trace the various simultaneous reactions. Contemplation of it was confusing. After long arguments, we often found ourselves in the ludicrous position of each having been converted to the other's side, with no more agreement than when the discussion began.

It was not till several months had passed, and every phase of the problem had been thrashed over and over, that the various reactions began to untangle themselves. When once a clear understanding had been obtained, there was no difficulty in designing suitable propellers, with proper diameter, pitch, and area of blade, to meet the requirements of the flyer. High efficiency in a screw-propeller is not dependent upon any particular or peculiar shape, and there is no such thing as a "best" screw. A propeller giving a high dynamic efficiency when used upon one machine, may be almost worthless when used upon another. The propeller should in every case be designed to meet the particular conditions of the machine to which it is to be applied. Our first propellers, built entirely from calculation, gave in useful work 66 per cent. of the power expended. This was about one third more than had been secured by Maxim or Langley.

The first flights with the power-machine were made on the 17th of December, 1903. Only five persons besides ourselves were present. These were Messrs. John T. Daniels, W. S. Dough, and A. D. Etheridge of the Kill Devil Life Saving Station; Mr. W. C. Brinkley of Manteo, and Mr. John Ward of Naghead. Although a general invitation had been extended to the people living within five or six miles, not many were willing to face the rigors of a cold December wind in order to see, as they no doubt thought, another flying-machine *not* fly. The first flight lasted only twelve seconds, a flight very modest compared with that of birds, but it was, nevertheless, the first in the history of the world in which a machine carrying a man had raised itself by its own power into the air in free flight, had sailed forward on a level course without reduction of speed, and had finally landed without being wrecked. The second and third flights were a little longer, and the fourth lasted fifty-nine seconds, covering a distance of 852 feet over the ground against a twenty-mile wind.

After the last flight, the machine was carried back to camp and set down in what was thought to be a safe place. But a few minutes later, while we were engaged in conversation about the flights, a sudden gust of wind struck the machine, and started to turn it over. All made a rush to stop it, but we were too late. Mr. Daniels, a giant in stature and strength, was lifted off his feet, and falling inside, between the surfaces, was shaken about like a rattle in a box as the machine rolled over and over. He finally fell out upon the sand with nothing worse than painful bruises, but the damage to the machine caused a discontinuance of experiments.

In the spring of 1904, through the kindness of Mr. Torrence Huffman of Dayton, Ohio, we were permitted to erect a shed, and to continue experiments, on what is known as the Huffman Prairie, at Simms Station, eight miles east of Dayton. The new machine was heavier and stronger, but similar to the one flown at Kill Devil Hill. When it was ready for its first trial, every newspaper in Dayton was notified, and about a dozen representatives of the press were present. Our only request was that no pictures be taken, and that the reports be unsensational, so as not to attract crowds to our experiment-grounds. There were probably fifty persons altogether on the ground. When preparations had been completed, a wind of only three or four miles was blowing,—insufficient for starting on so short a track,—but since many had come a long way to see the machine in action, an attempt was made. To add to the other difficulty, the engine refused to work properly. The machine, after running the length of the track, slid off the end without rising into the air at all. Several of the newspaper men returned the next day, but were again disappointed. The engine performed badly, and after a glide of only sixty feet, the machine came to the ground. Further trial was postponed till the motor could be put in better running condition. The reporters had now, no doubt, lost confidence in the machine, though their reports, in kindness, concealed it. Later, when they heard that we were making flights of several minutes' duration, knowing that longer flights had been made with air-ships, and not knowing any essential difference between air-ships and flying-machines, they were but little interested.

We had not been flying long in 1904 before we found that the problem of equilibrium had not as yet been entirely solved. Sometimes, in making a circle, the machine would turn over sidewise despite anything the operator could do, although, under the same conditions in ordinary straight flight, it could have been righted in an instant. In one flight, in 1905, while circling around a honey locust-tree at a height of about fifty feet, the machine suddenly began to turn up on one wing, and took a course toward the tree. The operator, not relishing the idea of landing in a thorn-tree, attempted to reach the ground. The left wing, however, struck the tree at a height of ten or twelve feet from the ground, and carried away several branches; but the flight, which had already covered a distance of six miles, was continued to the starting-point.

The causes of these troubles—too technical for explanation here—were not entirely overcome till the end of September, 1905. The flights then rapidly increased in length, till experiments were discontinued after the 5th of October, on account of the number of people attracted to the field. Although made on a ground open on every side, and bordered on two sides by much traveled thoroughfares, with electric cars passing every hour, and seen by all the people living in the neighborhood for miles around, and by several hundred others, yet these flights have been made by some newspapers the subject of a great "mystery."

A practical flyer having been finally realized, we spent the years 1906 and 1907 in constructing new machines and in business negotiations. It was not till May of this year that experiments (discontinued in October, 1905) were resumed at Kill Devil Hill, North Carolina. The recent flights were made to test the ability of our machine to meet the requirements of a contract with the United States Government to furnish a flyer capable of carrying two men and sufficient fuel supplies for a flight of 125 miles, with a speed of forty miles an hour. The machine used in these tests was the same one with which the flights were made at Simms Station in 1905, though several changes had been made to meet present requirements. The operator assumed a sitting position, instead of lying prone, as in 1905, and a seat was added for a passenger. A larger motor was installed, and radiators and gasolene reservoirs of larger capacity replaced those previously used. No attempt was made to make high or long flights.

In order to show the general reader the way in which the machine operates, let us fancy ourselves ready for the start. The machine is placed upon a single rail track facing the wind, and is securely fastened with a cable. The engine is put in motion, and the propellers in the rear whir.

You take your seat at the center of the machine beside the operator. He slips the cable, and you shoot forward. An assistant who has been holding the machine in balance on the rail, starts forward with you, but before you have gone fifty feet the speed is too great for him, and he lets go. Before reaching the end of the track the operator moves the front rudder, and the machine lifts from the rail like a kite supported by the pressure of the air underneath it. The ground under you is at first a perfect blur, but as you rise the objects become clearer. At a height of one hundred feet you feel hardly any motion at all, except for the wind which strikes your face. If you did not take the precaution to fasten your hat before starting, you have probably lost it by this time. The operator moves a lever: the right wing rises, and the machine swings about to the left. You make a very short turn, yet you do not feel the sensation of being thrown from your seat, so often experienced in automobile and railway travel. You find yourself facing toward the point from which you started. The objects on the ground now seem to be moving at much higher speed, though you perceive no change in the pressure of the wind on your face. You know then that you are traveling with the wind. When you near the starting-point, the operator stops the motor while still high in the air. The machine coasts down at an oblique angle to the ground, and after sliding fifty or a hundred feet comes to rest. Although the machine often lands when traveling at a speed of a mile a minute, you feel no shock whatever, and cannot, in fact, tell the exact moment at which it first touched the ground. The motor close beside you kept up an almost deafening roar during the whole flight, yet in your excitement, you did not notice it till it stopped!

Our experiments have been conducted entirely at our own expense. In the beginning we had no thought of recovering what we were expending, which was not great, and was limited to what we could afford for recreation. Later, when a successful flight had been made with a motor, we gave up the business in which we were engaged, to devote our entire time and capital to the development of a machine for practical uses. As soon as our condition is such that constant attention to business is not required, we expect to prepare for publication the results of our laboratory experiments, which alone made an early solution of the flying problem possible.